International Perspectives
on Social Security Reform

Also of interest from the Urban Institute Press

Social Security and the Family: Addressing Unmet Needs in an Underfunded System, edited by Melissa M. Favreault, Frank J. Sammartino, and C. Eugene Steuerle

Older and Wiser: The Economics of Public Pensions, by Lawrence H. Thompson

International Perspectives
on Social Security Reform

Edited by
Rudolph G. Penner

THE URBAN INSTITUTE PRESS
Washington, D.C.

THE URBAN INSTITUTE PRESS
2100 M Street, N.W.
Washington, D.C. 20037

Library of Congress Cataloging-in-Publication Data

International perspectives on social security reform / edited by Rudolph G. Penner.
        p. cm.
    Papers from a February 24, 2006 conference held by the Urban Institute to examine social security reform in six OECD countries
    Includes bibliographical references and index.
    ISBN 978-0-87766-743-8 (alk. paper)
    1.   Social security—OECD countries—Congresses.   2.   Retirement income—OECD countries—Congresses.   3.   Saving and investment—OECD countries—Congresses.   I. Penner, Rudolph Gerhard, 1936-
    HD7090.I6646   2007
    368.4'3—dc22

                                                            2007019923

Printed in the United States of America

14 13 12 11 10 09 08 07   1 2 3 4 5

THE URBAN INSTITUTE is a nonprofit, nonpartisan policy research and educational organization established in Washington, D.C., in 1968. Its staff investigates the social, economic, and governance problems confronting the nation and evaluates the public and private means to alleviate them. The Institute disseminates its research findings through publications, its web site, the media, seminars, and forums.

Through work that ranges from broad conceptual studies to administrative and technical assistance, Institute researchers contribute to the stock of knowledge available to guide decisionmaking in the public interest.

Conclusions or opinions expressed in Institute publications are those of the authors and do not necessarily reflect the views of officers or trustees of the Institute, advisory groups, or any organizations that provide financial support to the Institute.

Contents

Preface   ix

1 Canada   1
Réal Bouchard

COMMENTARY *Stuart Butler*   27
COMMENTARY *James C. Capretta*   31

2 Sweden   35
Agneta Kruse and Edward Palmer

COMMENTARY *Estelle James*   55
COMMENTARY *Lawrence H. Thompson*   61

3 Japan   69
Tetsuo Kabe

COMMENTARY *Jagadeesh Gokhale*   87
COMMENTARY *Richard Jackson*   91

4   Germany   97
     Michael Mersmann

     COMMENTARY *Maya MacGuineas*   103
     COMMENTARY *Neil Howe*   107

5   United Kingdom   111
     Alex Beer

     COMMENTARY *John Turner*   127
     COMMENTARY *Stanford G. Ross*   131

6   Italy   135
     Alicia Puente Cackley, Tom Moscovitch,
     and Benjamin Pfeiffer

     COMMENTARY *Paul N. Van de Water*   147
     COMMENTARY *Dalmer D. Hoskins*   151

     About the Editor   155

     About the Contributors   157

     Index   163

Preface

On February 24, 2006, the Urban Institute held a conference examining social security reform in six OECD countries. It was a time in which the social security debate in the United States seemed moribund. President George W. Bush had made some dramatic proposals in the previous year, but they were opposed vigorously by interest groups representing the elderly and by the Democratic party, and they gained little support elsewhere.

Yet, we know with certainty that the nation will have to return to this debate eventually. Our aging population combined with soaring health costs will create intolerable budget pressures within the next two decades. Although it is our health programs, Medicare and Medicaid, that will cause most of the problems, Social Security reform should be easier conceptually, if not politically. Consequently, exploring the varying approaches to social security reform in other democracies seemed interesting.

The good news is that reform is possible in a democracy, despite powerful opposing forces. The bad news is that in almost all the countries examined, reform had to wait until severe economic or budget problems, or both, arose. Such severe budget problems will not likely emerge in the United States for a decade or more, perhaps not until the 2020s.

Many countries have undertaken social security reform. In a variety of former Communist countries and in certain emerging economies, reform was necessary either because no system existed or because the system paid very low benefits. Replacing a defunct system with a more generous one is clearly much easier politically than cutting back on a functioning, generous system. For that reason, only developed countries with systems that functioned reasonably well prior to reform were chosen as subjects for the conference. Not all developed countries with interesting reforms could be accommodated, but those that were selected illustrate a wide variety of approaches. Conference papers were commissioned for Canada, Sweden, Japan, Germany, the United Kingdom, and Italy.

All countries represented have a more severely aging population than the United States. In some, such as Canada, the difference is slight, but in countries such as Japan and Italy, the population is aging extremely rapidly. In countries other than Canada and the UK, prereform public pensions were much more generous than in the United States, often providing much higher replacement rates at lower retirement ages. It is probably somewhat easier politically to cut back a highly generous system than one providing fairly low replacement rates.

The UK represented the most unusual case at the conference. Since its public pensions are price indexed and have eroded relative to the working population's standard of living, it is the only country now discussing an *increase* in its generosity. A commission has recommended that the UK adopt wage indexing, to be paid for by increasing the retirement age. Other countries' experiences suggest that the UK would make a huge mistake to do the former if it does not do the latter.

The UK has also taught the rest of the world valuable lessons in how not to implement individual accounts. The UK developed a system similar to that proposed by President Bush: individuals could opt out of the public system and obtain a payroll tax rebate to be invested privately. Here, the UK made two big mistakes. First, the information provided by the government to help people choose between private and public pensions underestimated changes in expected life, thus making the private approach appear more advantageous than it actually was. Second, sellers of mutual funds and of other private investments were not adequately regulated; overenthusiastic and outright dishonest salespeople advocated ill-advised investments. The Bush proposal avoided the latter problem by designing private accounts to resemble the civil service thrift plan, which offers a limited number of highly diversified, relatively safe investments. However, like the UK's approach, the Bush proposal may have been somewhat misleading. Cuts in traditional benefits were to repay deposits into the private accounts. The repayment carried a real interest rate of 3 percent. People may not have understood that the rate was probably higher than that which could be earned on a risk-free investment in inflation-indexed bonds or in a typical life-cycle fund.

The Canadian reform also had some unusual features. Canada decided to partially fund its pension system by increasing payroll taxes significantly—the rate went from 5.6 to 9.9 percent—and by depositing the resulting surplus into a pension trust fund. This fund could be invested in private assets to obtain higher returns. Because the pension system is a joint federal-provincial responsibility, the trust fund is entirely separate from the budgets of the federal government or the individual provinces. This makes it a good deal harder to use the trust fund indirectly to finance spending outside the pension system. Canada also created an independent board to be sure that investment decisions were not biased by political influences. Pension plan benefits were reduced somewhat by increasing the number of years in the benefit formula over which income is averaged, but the bulk of the reduction in Canada's long-run deficit came from the tax increase and the higher rate of return on their growing trust fund.

It is hard to imagine a similar reform in the United States. Americans would probably not tolerate such a significant increase in the payroll tax, and in many states, the so-called independent boards that invest state pension money have not been able to avoid responding to political pressures.

Most other countries represented in the conference started with payroll tax rates far higher than Canada's, and they faced the prospect of ever-increasing rates if the growth of benefits were not curbed. In Germany, Japan, and Italy, a series of reforms has decreased replacement rates and increased retirement ages. In Japan, reform has been aided by the fact that the system must be reviewed every five years and the legislature must respond when financial problems are reported.

Probably, the most interesting reform occurred in Sweden. They converted their defined benefit pay-as-you go system into something called a notional defined contribution system that is also pay-as-you-go. Tax payments accumulate in a paper (or notional) account, and an interest rate equal to the rate of wage growth is paid on the account balance. No real investment underlies these accounts. Upon retirement, the accumulated amount is converted into an annuity appropriate to a person's age at retirement and the life expectancy of his or her cohort. The Swedes avoided divisive debates about the appropriate retirement age and allowed people to retire at any time after age 61, but, of course, the later the retirement age, the higher the pension. The annuity assumes a real rate of return of

1.6 percent per year. If wages increase by a greater amount, annuities will increase and if by a smaller amount, annuities will decrease.

Note all of the automatic adjustments in the Swedish system. The system adjusts to changes in the rate of economic growth, because the interest rate paid on the notional defined contribution accounts is linked to wage growth, as is the generosity of the annuity. Changes in expected life are automatically considered when calculating the annuity. As if this were not enough protection against economic and demographic surprises, there is a further automatic adjustment: if the present value of the system's assets falls below the present value of its liabilities, the interest rate paid on accumulated balances and the benefits received by pensioners are automatically adjusted downward.

A funded individual account system was added to the pay-as-you-go system and will help offset some of the benefit reductions, compared to the benefits that were earlier promised. Investors are offered a complex choice of more than 700 mutual funds, but there is also a default investment that many choose.

Variants on the Swedish system have now been adopted in Italy and in some former Communist countries. That the system automatically gravitates toward sustainability is one reason for its appeal.

Canada, Japan, Germany, and Italy all have automatic mechanisms, similar to Sweden's, that reduce the growth of benefits when certain triggers are pulled. The triggers depend on economic or demographic variables, or on an actuarial review. Such mechanisms may be politically acceptable, because their effects are harder to predict than those of more explicit benefit cuts. Admittedly, most of the reforms considered in this conference are extremely complex and their implications may not have been clearly understood by most voters. This may be distressing to advocates of transparency in government, but it was certainly convenient politically.

During the social security debate in the United States, widespread agreement held that current retirees and those near retirement should not be affected by benefit cuts. (Near retirement was defined as being 55 and older.) Essentially, we could not reduce the rate of benefit growth and the associated benefits of compounding savings for 10 years. We might question this value judgment, because it is older generations who have benefited most from the current system. Also, the judgment created a major problem for the Bush proposals. The diversion of payroll taxes into individual accounts would have initially been paid for by borrowing and the borrowing would have lasted a long time—until cuts in traditional benefits gradually closed the deficit. The resulting accumulated debt could have been significantly smaller were benefit growth to be reduced sooner, by affecting the retired and the nearly retired.

The countries represented in the conference treated the already retired very differently. Japan and Italy reduced their promised benefits significantly while Canada and Sweden were fairly lenient, although the already retired could be affected by the automatic balancing mechanisms.

Different countries used different political approaches to reform. In Canada, the provinces' important role in the pension system meant that the federal ruling party had to cooperate with the different parties ruling the provinces. There was no choice but to be multipartisan. In Sweden, a parliamentary committee of seven parties worked on the reform and in the end, five of the parties agreed to move forward. In the United States, it is not likely that progress could be made without bipartisan cooperation. Our recent debate was hampered when President Bush's opponents did not put forward proposals of their own, so it was hard to start a bargaining process that could have led to reform.

In Italy, the legislature delegated the responsibility for designing reforms to the Ministry of Finance. Only a wild dreamer could imagine such an approach in the United States.

Although other countries must be congratulated for undertaking painful and therefore courageous reforms, to say that all have permanently solved their problems would be an exaggeration. In all cases, the automatic balancing mechanisms are relatively new and have not yet gone into effect. If any of the triggers are pulled, the political reaction will be interesting. In some countries, the reforms will take effect slowly and perseverance will be necessary. That is particularly true in Italy, with its 10-year phase-in period. (Unfortunately, while benefit costs remain high, Italy will require a payroll tax rate of over 30 percent—a severe drag on employment.) Most countries also face unresolved problems related to rising health costs, a problem that is much more severe in the United States than the problem posed by our social security system.

Yet, an American cannot help but be envious of the progress made abroad. We can only hope that we can make similar progress, but without the budget and economic traumas that spurred reform in other countries. I think that the lessons for American legislators are clear. First, progress here, without the cooperation of the major political parties that characterized the Swedish and Canadian reforms, is impossible. Second, once the reform debate begins, we can consider options that imply a radical change in the structure of the Social Security program. Third, America would be wise to buttress reforms with automatic mechanisms that ensure the program will be sustainable, if the demographic and economic assumptions underlying reform turn out to be less favorable than expected. All in all, the Swedish reform has some attractive features, especially the many provisions that automatically ensure sustainability, and should be considered when the reform debate resumes in the United States.

1

Canada

Réal Bouchard

In the mid-1990s, the Canada Pension Plan (CPP), one of the three pillars of Canada's retirement income system, was about to experience serious financial difficulties. Its affordability and financial sustainability were in jeopardy. In fact, the CPP—an earnings-related social insurance plan providing retirement, disability, and survivor benefits—was facing a two-and-a-half-fold increase in contribution rates by 2030.

To address this situation, significant changes were made to restore the CPP's health. The 1997 CPP reforms moved the plan from essentially a pay-as-you-go system to partial prefunding, and created the CPP Investment Board (CPPIB), at arm's length from Canada's governments, to invest plan assets in a diversified portfolio of marketable securities.

Structure of the Canadian Retirement Income System

Canada's retirement income system consists of three pillars: the first two, the Canada Pension Plan and the Old Age Security program, are the system's public components; tax-assisted private savings constitute the third pillar (table 1.1).

The CPP provides a basic taxable, earnings-related pension to all workers in Canada excluding Québec's, who are covered by the Québec Pension Plan (QPP).[1] The CPP is financed by contributions from employees and employers on earnings between the yearly basic exemption (C$3,500) and the yearly maximum pensionable earnings (C$42,100 in 2006, linked to the average industrial wage), and by investment earnings on excess contributions (i.e., contributions not immediately required by the plan to pay benefits). The contribution rate is 9.9 percent, split equally between employees and employers. Self-employed workers pay the combined rate.

The CPP retirement benefit is relatively modest. The replacement rate is 25 percent of a worker's average pensionable earnings over his working life, where wages are indexed to the increase in Canada's average industrial wage over that period. In 2006, the maximum benefit at age 65 was C$10,135 annually, or 25 percent of C$40,540 (the average of maximum pensionable earnings in the five preceding years). In addition to retirement benefits, which comprise approximately 70 percent of the expenditures, the plan also provides disability, survivor, and children's benefits, along with a lump-sum death benefit to the estate. Disability and survivor benefits include a flat-rate component as well as an earnings-related amount, and therefore serve a greater redistributive role than the retirement benefit.

The other pillar in the public pension system is the Old Age Security (OAS) program, which provides a basic yearly benefit (C$5,816 in 2006) for all seniors 65 and older who meet the residence requirements and whose annual income is below C$62,144 (benefits are reduced by 15 percent of income in excess of C$62,144). In addition, the program provides the Guaranteed Income Supplement (GIS), targeted at seniors with low incomes (36 percent of OAS recipients receive it). Combined, the OAS and GIS provide maximum annual benefits (in 2006) of C$12,944 and C$20,983 for singles and couples, respectively (Government of Canada 2006c). OAS and GIS expenditures represent about 2.2 percent of gross domestic product (GDP) (Office of the Superintendent 2005) and 24 percent of the Government of Canada's transfers to persons and other levels of government (Government of Canada 2005b).

Canada also has a well-developed private pillar, consisting of tax-assisted private savings, including employer-sponsored Registered Pension Plans (RPPs) and individual Registered Retirement Savings Plans (RRSPs).

In 2003, OAS/GIS benefits accounted for about 32 percent of Canada's retirement income system to Canadians age 65 and older; CPP retirement benefits, 25 percent; and RPPs/RRSPs, about 43 percent.[2] Together the three pillars help achieve the main goals of the Canadian retirement income system: to prevent poverty among seniors by providing them with a guaranteed minimum income, and to help Canadians maintain their

Table 1.1. The Three Pillars of the Canadian Retirement Income System

	Description	Eligibility	Financing
Public pillar			
Canada Pension Plan/Québec Pension Plan (CPP/QPP)	Annual maximum of C$10,135, or 25 percent of average pensionable earnings Survivor and disability benefits also available A lump-sum death benefit is payable to the worker's estate	All workers contributing through earnings Payable as early as age 60 at a reduced rate, or in full at age 65	Investment earnings + employer/ee contributions (9.9 percent split equally) on earnings between C$3,500 and C$42,100 (wage indexed) Price indexed annually
Old Age Security (OAS)	Annual maximum of C$5,816, reduced when income from other sources reaches C$62,144 and eliminated if income is over C$100,914	All seniors meeting residence requirements[a]	General Government of Canada revenues Price indexed quarterly
Guaranteed Income Supplement (GIS)[b]	Singles: annual maximum of C$7,128, reduced by C$1 for every C$2 of other income (excluding OAS) Couples: annual maximum of C$9,352	Low-income seniors receiving OAS	General Government of Canada revenues Price indexed quarterly
Private pillar			
Tax-assisted and other private savings (e.g., Registered Pension Plans [RPPs] and individual Registered Retirement Savings Plans [RRSPs])	Annual contribution limit of C$19,000 for RPPs and C$18,000 for RRSPs Reduces taxable income, but withdrawal taxable	All workers, through their employers	Individuals and their employers

Source: Government of Canada (2005a; 2006a, b, c).

Notes: C$ amounts are for January to March 2006. A senior is defined as a person at least 65 years old.

a. To be eligible for the OAS, recipients must be Canadian citizens and must have lived in Canada for 40 years. Those who reside in Canada for fewer than 40 years but more than 10 years will receive partial OAS benefits prorated by the number of years of residence. In addition, an Allowance component is payable to those age 60 to 64 who are married to a pensioner or who are the survivor of a pensioner. See this chapter's appendix for more details.

b. GIS is a supplement to OAS. Approximately 36 percent of seniors who receive OAS also receive some GIS.

living standards in retirement. Public pensions (OAS, GIS, and the CPP/
QPP) replace significant income for low- and modest-income earners
(i.e., from 75 to over 100 percent of preretirement earnings for singles
who earned on average C$20,000 or less) and about 45 percent for
those earning an average income (roughly C$40,000).[3] Middle- and
higher-income earners must accumulate additional savings in RPPs
and RRSPs to achieve replacement rates of 50 to 70 percent; contribution limits are set high enough to allow Canadians to do this. Many
Canadians take advantage of these vehicles—approximately 61 percent
of tax filers older than 65 reported income from either RPPs or RRSPs.[4]
Furthermore, many seniors supplement their RPPs or RRSPs with
income from other sources (e.g., wages, marketable securities, or rental
income).

Comparison to the U.S. Retirement Income System

Total public pension expenditures as a percentage of GDP are similar in
Canada and the United States—about 4.6 and 4.3 percent, respectively[5]—
but the structure of benefits under the two systems varies. The CPP bears
some similarity to the Old-Age, Survivors, and Disability Insurance
(OASDI) program in the United States—both are contributory plans providing retirement, survivor, and disability benefits. However, in the CPP,
the primary insurance formula does not vary with earnings, and benefits
are available earlier and not reduced for earnings.[6] The CPP contribution
rate is lower and insurance is provided on a much narrower range of earnings. The CPP is also a much smaller program, with benefit expenditures
totaling 2.4 percent of GDP, compared to 4.3 percent of GDP for the
OASDI program in 2005 (Government of Québec 2006; Office of the
Superintendent 2004).[7] Supplemental Security Income (SSI) is the broad
equivalent to the Canadian GIS program but much smaller; benefit
expenditures to those age 65 or older are less than 0.03 percent of GDP
compared to about 0.5 percent for the GIS (Office of the Superintendent
2005; U.S. Social Security Administration 2005a). There is no equivalent
to the Canadian OAS program in the United States. This said, the variable
primary insurance formula of the OASDI retirement benefit fulfills some
of the same redistributive functions as the OAS in Canada.

Figure 1.1 shows benefits (in US$) based on annual preretirement
earnings for a single senior under both public pension systems. For

Figure 1.1. Replacement Rates of Retirement Income for Single Seniors, Canada and the United States, 2006

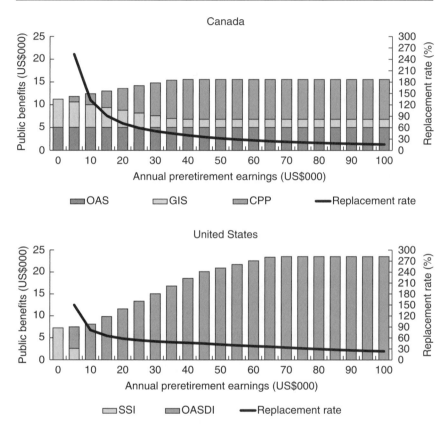

Source: Department of Finance Canada calculations (2006).

Notes: The figure assumes no private savings, and uses a retirement age of 65 for both Canada and the United States (i.e., for simplicity, U.S. amounts do not take into account reductions based on age of take-up). Amounts for Canada have been converted to U.S. currency using the nominal noon exchange rate on January 3, 2006 (i.e., US$1.00/C$1.1571).

CPP = Canada Pension Plan

GIS = Guaranteed Income Supplement

OAS = Old Age Security

OASDI = Old-Age, Survivors, and Disability Insurance

SSI = Supplemental Security Income

simplicity, the figure assumes no private sources of retirement income—an extreme assumption, particularly at higher preretirement income levels. Nonetheless, the figure illustrates several points. Notably, compared to the CPP, the OASDI has a greater redistributive role: it provides a higher ratio of benefits to earnings for those who had low preretirement earnings. In Canada, the redistributive role is delivered through the OAS program. Second, while the Canadian public system has a much higher replacement rate for individuals with low income (i.e., about 150 percent in Canada for a single senior with average preretirement earnings of $10,000, compared to about 80 percent in the United States[8]), the United States has a higher replacement rate for middle- to high-income earners.

Financing of the Public Pension Plans

CPP

CPP expenditures are financed by contributions paid into the plan by employees, their employers, and the self-employed, and from income earned on excess contributions (i.e., contributions not immediately required by the plan to pay benefits.)

Since the CPP was established in 1966, its financial activities (revenue and expenditure flows) have not been part of a reporting entity in the Government of Canada's public accounts. This is because the CPP is under the joint control of the Government of Canada and the provinces. While the legislation governing the CPP is federal, the federal government requires the formal consent of the provinces to amend it.[9] CPP assets are not included as assets in the Government of Canada's public accounts. However, any borrowing from the CPP by the Government of Canada is recorded as a liability of the Government of Canada (i.e., included in total central government debt).

OAS/GIS

The financial activities of the OAS/GIS program form part of the public accounts of the Government of Canada. Both programs are financed from federal government revenues (i.e., no premiums) and hence, impact the government's fiscal position directly.

Pressures for Reform

The CPP was established in 1966 as a pay-as-you-go pension plan with a small contingency reserve invested solely in nonmarketable long-term provincial government bonds at below-market rates (with the Government of Canada as the default borrower).[10] At inception, the combined employer-employee contribution rate was set at a modest 3.6 percent of contributory earnings, and the plan's architects expected Canadians and their employers would never have to pay more than 5.5 percent of earnings to the CPP.

By the early 1980s, it became clear that these projections were off track, principally because demographic and economic conditions had fundamentally changed since the plan's inception. Expenditures, expressed as a percentage of contributory earnings—the pay-as-you-go rate—were expected to rise significantly to reach 12 percent by 2030. In 1986, CPP stewards responded by setting a new rolling 25-year schedule of contribution-rate increases that would provide for a contingency reserve of two years of benefits. The combined employer-employee contribution rate of 3.6 percent, in place since 1966, would gradually rise to 7.6 percent by 2011. In 1991, the 25-year contribution rate schedule was extended by five years, and a contribution rate of 10.1 percent was projected by 2016.

The 15th Actuarial Report on the CPP, released in February 1995, projected that the plan's contingency reserve would be depleted by 2015 and that the scheduled 2016 contribution rate of 10.1 percent would not yield sufficient revenues to pay plan benefits in that year. Furthermore, it estimated that under the existing benefit structure, the contribution rate would have had to increase to 14.2 percent by 2030 to cover escalating costs (Office of the Superintendent 1995).

The release of the actuarial report precipitated a strong reaction and widespread concern about the plan's future. In spite of the significant increases in premiums—from 3.6 percent in 1986 to 10.1 percent in 2016—the projection that the plan would be unable to pay all benefits in 2016 proved difficult to ignore.

Within a few weeks the federal government, through its 1995 budget, stated its commitment to providing Canadians with a fair and sustainable retirement income system. The regular five-year review of the CPP by federal and provincial finance ministers, which was to start that fall, would take the actuarial report's findings under serious consideration. As part of the review, for the first time ever, the governments decided to launch major public consultations to get Canadians' views on what they wanted from the CPP. To assist them, the federal and provincial governments released in February 1996 *An Information Paper for Consultations on the Canada Pension Plan* (Federal/Provincial/Territorial Governments 1996), which outlined the challenges facing the CPP in the coming years.

In short, the information paper highlighted the fundamental problem: expenditures, expressed as pay-as-you-go rates, were getting out of control. They had grown much more rapidly than expected and were projected to escalate even more dramatically in the future. Four factors were largely responsible for driving up CPP costs:

- changing demographics (i.e., the decline in the ratio of contributors to beneficiaries due to the aging population);
- changing economic conditions, including slower earnings growth and higher real interest rates (which made prefunding the plan more attractive);
- benefit enrichments since the mid-1970s; and
- rapid growth in disability benefit expenditures in the previous decade (i.e., a 93 percent increase in CPP disability beneficiaries from 1986–1987 to 1995–1996), due to looser eligibility criteria and plan administration.

The information paper included a number of options to reduce costs and change how the plan was to be financed, so future contribution rates would not have to rise to 14 percent. It also stressed that continuing with pay-as-you-go financing would ultimately mean large increases in premiums that would most affect the generation of workers following the baby boom.

With the release of the information paper, Canadians had the opportunity to make educated assessments of the program and form their own opinions. Public consultations, guided by panels of federal and provincial elected representatives, were held in all provinces, over a period of two months. These revealed broad (though not unanimous) support for the CPP's fundamental character as a public defined benefit pension.[11] That said, requiring future generations to pay contribution rates of 14 percent for a plan that provided relatively modest benefits was deemed unacceptable by most, and many Canadians appeared to accept that current workers should pay a fairer share of the benefits they would receive. Canadians voiced broad support for significant changes in the CPP's financing and investment policy and, not surprisingly, strong resistance to a substantial reduction in benefits.

Using the consultation results (published in June 1996), the 15th Actuarial Report, and a lot of determination, federal and provincial finance ministers worked extensively on a reform package that would permanently "fix" the CPP. The public pressure and the perceived—and actual—crisis provided the political motivation necessary for all parties to work together.

The Reform Agreement

The federal and provincial governments reached an agreement on a reform package in February 1997: a three-pronged approach to restoring the financial sustainability of the CPP (Government of Canada 1997). First, the plan would move from essentially a pay-as-you-go system (with a small contingency reserve) to partial prefunding (at about 25 percent of the present value of liabilities) by accelerating the already-scheduled contribution rate increases—the contribution rate would increase to 9.9 percent by 2003 from 5.6 percent in 1996, and the contributory base would be broadened as well (i.e., by freezing the basic earnings exemption at $3,500 rather than continuing to wage index it). Second, the plan would adopt a new investment policy to improve the return on CPP assets, and an independent board would manage these assets. Third, measures would be taken to slow the growth in benefit expenditures, especially disability benefits. Benefits already being paid as of December 31, 1997, would be grandfathered.

Fuller Funding

Raising contribution rates more quickly to a level that could be maintained over the next 75 years—to 9.9 percent from 2003 onward—was viewed to be the fairest way to equalize the CPP's costs across generations. This stable contribution rate would cover the costs of each contributor's own benefits, plus a share of the "unfunded" burden that had built up because both current and past contributors had paid far less than their benefits were worth. Presently working Canadians would therefore pay a fairer share of CPP costs. This new financing approach would ease some of the contribution burden that would otherwise be passed on to future generations of workers.

Increasing the contribution rate and broadening the contributory base would allow the plan to build a larger reserve fund. It would grow from less than two years of annual benefit expenditures in 1997 to nearly five years over the following two decades, and remain at this level until the end of the 75-year projection period. A portion of the fund's investment earnings would help pay benefits when contribution revenues would no longer be sufficient to cover expenditures, after the large baby boom cohort retires.[12] In the absence of these investment earnings, plan expenditures would have to be covered by higher contributions.

A New Investment Policy

The second key element of the reform was the new investment policy. It provided that CPP contributions not immediately required for paying benefits be transferred to a new independent government agency—the CPP Investment Board (CPPIB)—and managed professionally, like other major Canadian public and private pension investment funds (i.e., in a diversified portfolio of marketable foreign and domestic assets in the best interests of plan members, without undue risk of loss[13]). Under this policy, the plan was expected to earn a higher long-term real return of 3.8 percent, compared to the 2.5 percent it was earning with the non-market, largely provincial government bond portfolio. Initially, the bond portfolio, along with a cash balance equivalent to three months of expenditures, was left with the Government of Canada to manage. These assets were transferred to the CPPIB in 2004 when additional legislation came into force.[14]

The CPPIB's independence is assured through its mandate as well as its robust governance structure, both of which are set out in legislation. The mandate gives the CPPIB fiduciary responsibility for plan investments, and requires it to act prudently and in the plan members' best interests. In addition, the CPPIB is subject to the same investment regulations as all other pension plans in Canada, and is insulated from political influence. The governance structure requires that the federal and provincial ministers appoint knowledgeable professional directors, with candidates screened and selected by a nominating committee.

Changes to Benefits and Their Administration

Finally, a number of changes were made to the calculation of all benefits and to eligibility for and administration of the disability benefit. For retirement pensions, the formula for indexing earnings would now be based on the last five years of maximum pensionable earnings, instead of the last three. For disability pensions, eligibility would now require workers to have a longer and more recent labor force attachment. Administration was also tightened, for example, by no longer considering applicants' socioeconomic characteristics in determining work capacity. In addition, retirement pensions for disability beneficiaries would now be based on maximum pensionable earnings at the time the disability occurs (instead of when the recipient turns 65), and then price indexed to age 65. The lump-sum death benefit would also be reduced to six months of retirement benefits up to a maximum of $2,500, and frozen.

The 15th Actuarial Report projected that these changes would reduce total annual benefit expenditures by almost 10 percent in 2030, compared to what they otherwise would have been.

Financial Implications to Reform

Canada's chief actuary estimated that the proposed reform would shave about 4 percentage points off the CPP's long-term cost. Rather than having to increase to more than 14 percent in 2030, the contribution rate would not exceed 9.9 percent from 2003 onward.[15] The 15th Actuarial Report estimated that the revenue measures (bringing forward the already-scheduled increases in contribution rates and broadening of the contributory base) accounted for about half the reduction in the long-term contribution rate. The new investment policy and the reduction in benefits each accounted for 1 percentage point in savings to contributors.

Factors in the Reform's Success

Why was the CPP reform successful? After all, many of the plan's structural issues were evident as early as a decade before the reform. Over this period, however, the political and public will to address these issues was not present. By the mid-1990s, however, a number of factors crystallized to facilitate reform.

The Right Timing

Behind the political will to reform the CPP was the need for fiscal restraint and deficit reduction faced by all governments in the 1990s, which served as a backdrop to the actuarial report that signaled the plan's future insolvency. By 1993, the Government of Canada's debt had climbed to 70 percent of GDP, up from 18 percent in less than two decades. Over a third of federal revenues were required to service this debt, of which nearly half was external debt. There was growing concern in international financial markets that this situation could not continue.

In early 1994, the Government of Canada embarked on a sustained effort to improve its finances. Between 1994 and the time of the CPP reform agreement, several federal budgets focused on deficit reduction and on stabilizing, then bringing down, the debt-to-GDP ratio. Doing otherwise would have been unfair to future generations and possibly undermined growth in living standards. The CPP's financial problems could be cast in a policy context of general fiscal restraint accepted by decision-makers and the public. Both understood and agreed that changes were unavoidable, that delaying action would simply increase the magnitude of future adjustments, that failure to act would create uncertainty and instability, and that protection for seniors should be fair and sustainable for younger generations.

Public Consultations

This discourse on fairness and the risks of inaction was central to the CPP Information Paper. The resulting public consultations provided guidance as to the criteria that should determine if proposed changes were desirable and acceptable.

Fair Financing

The paper specifically asked Canadians whether continuing with pay-as-you-go financing was fair. A large majority of participants thought that it was not (Federal/Provincial/Territorial CPP Consultations Secretariat 1996). They also appeared to accept that the current generation of workers, who benefited from the lower contribution rates of the past, should pay a "fairer share" of their own benefits and not pass an excessive burden to future generations.

The Plan's Public Nature

Most participants in the consultations did not advocate privatizing the CPP or creating mandatory individual accounts. The limited support for privatization stemmed in part from concerns about financing the plan's outstanding unfunded liabilities, which were then estimated to be in excess of C$550 billion. Privatizing the CPP and honoring outstanding obligations would mean asking the next generation (or two) to pay twice—for the new CPP as well as for past outstanding obligations. This would be unfair; hence, the main reason for the governments to employ a stable long-term contribution rate that would spread the cost of outstanding obligations over all future generations.

A Package Approach

Based on the consultations' results, for any significant change to contribution rates and benefits to be widely accepted and successful, a series of other measures had to be taken—notably, a new higher-return investment policy at arm's length from the governments, and stronger governance and accountability.

A New Investment Policy

Consultations brought to the fore public concerns about how the governments were handling the CPP. The new investment policy proved crucial to sealing support for the reforms and assuring the public that higher contribution rates and changes in benefits would fix the plan for good. Having plan assets invested at arm's length from the governments in a diversified portfolio of marketable assets also provided confidence that the assets would be well managed.

The political will to consider a market investment policy for the CPP emerged partly because borrowing from the plan was not a significant source of funds for the Government of Canada. In 1996, total Government of Canada debt held by the CPP amounted to C$3.5 billion, or less than 1 percent of its total outstanding market debt. The sporadic availability of CPP funds to the federal government reduced further its importance as a source of funds.

CPP borrowing was more important for the provinces, acting as a source of subsidized funds. To facilitate the move to a market investment policy, the provinces were allowed to roll over existing borrowing for one additional 20-year term.[16] However, the rollover would be at prevailing market interest rates. That the provinces were willing to accept this reflects their limited dependence on the CPP for off-budget borrowing, their recognition of the need for policy integrity, and the pivotal role of the new market investment policy in the agreement.

Stronger Plan Governance and Accountability

Three particular improvements to CPP governance and accountability reassured the public that plan stewards would act responsibly in the future. First, actuarial reporting would be increased to every three years from every five. This would ensure that any problems were promptly brought to policymakers' attention. Second, new default provisions in the CPP legislation would result in speedy corrective action, were a review to reveal that the legislated contribution rate could not sustain the plan indefinitely and the ministers could not agree how to address this situation.[17] Third, other new provisions would require that any future benefit improvements be fully funded. This would prevent enrichments being made without proper adjustments in contribution rates, as in the past.

Federal-Provincial Decisionmaking

The CPP's joint federal-provincial nature was instrumental in holding the agreement together once it had been reached, although it also likely contributed to the delay in reaching a reform consensus before the late 1990s. Once an agreement had been reached, the federal-provincial process allowed the political cost of the agreement to be spread across two orders of government. It also limited public criticism of the agreement. Similarly, it meant that failure to reform the plan and ensure its long-term viability would have been blamed jointly on the federal and provincial governments.

The agreement's joint federal-provincial nature also made its passage through the legislature easier than may otherwise have been the case. Any significant changes to proposed legislation could unravel the agreement. As a result, the amending bill passed through the parliamentary process with no significant changes. At the same time, Québec introduced a series of measures to reform the QPP that were similar to the changes being

made to the CPP. That both plans were overhauled at the same time rein-
forced the perception that these changes were necessary.

The CPP Today

The 1997 reforms have been successful in restoring the CPP's financial sustainability. The most recent actuarial report (Office of the Superintendent
2004) has confirmed that the 9.9 percent contribution rate is sufficient to
ensure the plan's financial sustainability for at least the next 75 years (the
projection period used in CPP actuarial reports). A panel of three independent actuaries, chosen through an arm's length selection process, has
reviewed the actuarial report and found its assumptions, methods, and
conclusions to be robust. The federal and provincial governments have
committed to independent reviews and their publication. Canadians can
have confidence in the CPP's actuarial projections.[18]

After some six years of operation, the CPPIB has evolved into a world-
class investment corporation with a major presence in Canadian and
global capital markets. At the end of December 2005, total assets under
CPPIB management were valued at C$92.5 billion (i.e., 6.8 percent of
GDP). They consisted of publicly traded stocks (56.6 percent), government bonds (29.7 percent), real return assets (8.4 percent), private equities (4.3 percent), and cash and money market securities (1.0 percent), and
included both foreign and domestic assets (Canada Pension Plan Investment Board 2006). With transfer of the government bond portfolio to the
CPPIB being completed in spring 2007, the Investment Board now man-
ages the entirety of CPP assets.

In 2005, the annual return on total CPP assets was 8.5 percent (17.6 percent in 2004) and the five-year average real rate of return was 4.5 percent
(Canada Pension Plan Investment Board 2005). The most recent actuarial report projects a 4.1 percent long-term real rate of return on CPP assets.
This is consistent with historical yields for large pension plans. From 2005
to 2025, real rates of return are expected to be slightly higher. By 2010, CPP
assets of C$147 billion are projected and by 2022, they are expected to
cover nearly 25 percent of the plan's actuarial liabilities (Office of the
Superintendent 2004). By this time, a portion of investment earnings will
be used to finance projected benefit expenditures that otherwise would
have to be paid through higher contributions.

Conclusions

In recent years, a number of international organizations (e.g., the World Bank, the OECD) have ranked the public component of Canada's retirement income system highly, in offering an adequate retirement income while maintaining affordability and sustainability as the population ages. As one of the system's two public pillars, the CPP, particularly after the major reforms in 1997, has contributed to these positive assessments.

The path to reforming the CPP was not always clear. But our success is. Through the 1997 reforms, the governments were able to preserve the CPP's fundamental character—a public defined benefit pension plan—while ensuring its long-term affordability for (and fairness to) future generations. Canadians said this was important. The governments delivered.

As importantly, the 1997 reforms established robust tools to deal with unexpected future events—because we know the future is uncertain. More frequent actuarial reporting will bring problems to light earlier, new default provisions will ensure rapid policy action to address potential problems, and the new full-funding provisions for benefit enrichments will ensure that their cost is not passed to future generations. As a result of these governance changes, the CPP should be able to weather the uncertain future. This too is a success.

What can other countries learn from Canada's experience? Our experience suggests that the "right" conditions are necessary to move forward with pension plan reform. What these conditions are will vary, depending on the country. When they are present, however, they will contribute to a strong consensus that a problem exists and needs to be fixed. They may also guide the nature of the reform agenda.

Well-directed broad-based public consultations were also crucial in framing a reform package that federal and provincial governments could agree on and that Canadians could support. The consultations demonstrated that Canadians did not want a band-aid solution. Had the CPP reform package not addressed the plan's long-term financial health and not included such key elements as the arm's length investment policy, the federal and provincial governments would not likely have reached an agreement.

Finally, a public pension's significance as a source of retirement income will influence a country's ability to reform. The relatively modest benefit provided by the CPP, as well as the strong sense that it was first and foremost a retirement plan with benefits that should be linked to contributions, likely made reform easier. For public pension programs that attempt to address a number of objectives, and with higher replacement rates, reform may be more difficult.

NOTES

This chapter was prepared with the assistance of Suzan Kalinowski and Julie Cain.

1. The parallel Québec Pension Plan is managed and administered by the Government of Québec, but provides similar benefits and has the same contributory requirements as the CPP.

2. Calculations by Finance Canada using Canada Revenue Agency 2003 data (Canada Revenue Agency 2005).

3. Calculations by Finance Canada.

4. Calculations by Finance Canada using Canada Revenue Agency 2003 data (Canada Revenue Agency 2005).

5. Based on Government of Québec (2005), Office of the Superintendent (2003, 2004), and U.S. Social Security Administration (2005a, b). The U.S. percentage (estimated) includes Old-Age, Survivors, and Disability Insurance and only the proportion of Supplemental Security Income expenditures for individuals age 65 or older.

6. In 2006, OASDI primary insurance for an individual who receives his benefit at the normal retirement age is the sum of 90 percent on the first US$656 of average indexed monthly earnings (AIME), 32 percent on the next US$3,299 of AIME, and 15 percent on AIME above US$3,955. The maximum monthly benefit for this individual is US$2,053. The normal retirement age in 2006 (for the cohort born in 1941) is 65 years and eight months.

7. The CPP figure includes Québec Pension Plan expenditures.

8. Calculations by Finance Canada.

9. In return for a constitutional amendment to allow federal incursion in an area of provincial responsibility (disability pensions), the federal government granted provinces joint control over the CPP. Changes to contributions, benefits, investment policy, and financing require the formal consent of at least two-thirds of the provinces (representing at least two-thirds of the population) to have the force of law.

10. Provinces' access to these funds was based on the proportion of contributions made by their residents. Any funds not subscribed by the provinces would be borrowed by the Government of Canada at an interest rate based on the average yield to maturity of outstanding Government of Canada long-term obligations (i.e., the same rate available to provinces).

11. Some submissions to the consultation argued for replacing the CPP with a system of individual accounts, although they were a minority.

12. The most recent actuarial report projects this will be in 2022. By 2050, about 12 percent of total expenditures will be funded by investment earnings (Office of the Superintendent 2004).

13. Currently, 31.7 percent of the CPPIB portfolio is invested in foreign assets (Canada Pension Plan Investment Board 2005). Limits on foreign asset holdings by tax-deferred retirement savings vehicles were eliminated in 2005.

14. Transfer of the bond portfolio had occurred over three years and will be completed in spring 2007. Further details can be found in Office of the Superintendent (2002) and in the amending bill, Bill C-3 (House Government, 37th Parliament, 2nd Session, 2006).

15. See Office of the Superintendent (1997). Actuarial projections are for 75 years.

16. The Government of Canada was not provided a rollover option.

17. The default provisions included a freeze on benefit indexation and an automatic increase in the contribution rate until the subsequent review or a decision by ministers to address the CPP's long-term health.

18. Actuarial projections for the CPP are undertaken by the Office of the Chief Actuary (OCA), which reports to the Superintendent of Financial Institutions, a senior civil servant responsible for regulating deposit-taking institutions, insurance companies, and federally regulated employer-sponsored pension plans. CPP actuarial projections are based on "best estimate" assumptions of future demographic and economic experience, and include sensitivity analysis. For more information, please refer to the OCA web site (http://www.osfi-bsif.gc.ca/osfi/index_e.aspx?DetailID=498).

REFERENCES

Canada Pension Plan Investment Board. 2005. *Annual Report 2005.* Toronto: Canada Pension Plan Investment Board. http://www.cppib.ca/info/annual/ar_2005.pdf. (Accessed February 15, 2007.)

————. 2006. "CPP Reserve Fund Grows to $92.5 Billion." News Release, February 8. Toronto: Canada Pension Plan Investment Board. http://www.cppib.ca/News_Room/News_Releases/nr_02080601.html. (Accessed February 15, 2007.)

Canada Revenue Agency. 2005. *Final Statistics: Sample Data, 2005 Edition (2003 Tax Year).* Ottawa: Canada Revenue Agency. http://www.cra-arc.gc.ca/agency/stats/gb03/pst/final/menu-e.html. (Accessed February 15, 2007.)

Federal/Provincial/Territorial CPP Consultations Secretariat. 1996. *Report on the Canada Pension Plan Consultations.* Ottawa: Department of Finance Canada. http://www.fin.gc.ca/cpp/finrep/cpp-e.pdf. (Accessed February 15, 2007.)

Federal/Provincial/Territorial Governments of Canada. 1996. *An Information Paper for Consultations on the Canada Pension Plan.* Ottawa: Department of Finance Canada. http://www.fin.gc.ca/cpp/maindoc/cppe.pdf. (Accessed February 15, 2007.)

Government of Canada. 1997. *Securing the Canada Pension Plan: Agreement on Proposed Changes to the CPP.* Ottawa: Department of Finance Canada. http://www.fin.gc.ca/cpp/sec/secure.pdf. (Accessed February 15, 2007.)

————. 2005a. *Budget 2005.* Ottawa: Department of Finance Canada. http://www.fin.gc.ca/budget05/bp/bpc4de.htm. (Accessed February 15, 2007.)

————. 2005b. *Public Accounts of Canada 2005, Volume I.* Ottawa: Public Works and Government Services Canada. http://epe.lac-bac.gc.ca/100/201/301/public_accounts_can/2005/v1pa05-e.pdf. (Accessed February 15, 2007.)

————. 2006a. "Canada Pension Plan (CPP)." Ottawa: Human Resources and Social Development Canada. http://www.hrsdc.gc.ca/en/isp/cpp/cpptoc.shtml. (Accessed February 15, 2007.)

———. 2006b. "Canada Pension Plan Financing." Ottawa: Department of Finance Canada. http://www.fin.gc.ca/cpp/indexe.html. (Accessed February 15, 2007.)

———. 2006c. "Old Age Security (OAS)." Ottawa: Human Resources and Social Development Canada. http://www.hrsdc.gc.ca/en/isp/oas/oastoc.shtml. (Accessed February 15, 2007.)

———. 2006d. "Monthly Statistical Bulletins." Ottawa: Human Resources and Social Development Canada. http://www.hrsdc.gc.ca/en/isp/statistics/monthly.shtml. (Accessed February 15, 2007.)

Government of Québec, Régie des Rentes. 2005. "The Québec Pension Plan." Québec: Régie des Rentes. http://www.rrq.gouv.qc.ca/en/programmes/regime_rentes/. (Accessed February 15, 2007.)

———. 2006. "Actuarial Report of the Québec Pension Plan." Québec: Régie des Rentes. http://www.rrq.gouv.qc.ca/en/services/publications/regime_rentes/analyse_actuarielle_2003.htm. (Accessed February 15, 2007.)

Office of the Superintendent of Financial Institutions Canada. 1995. *Canada Pension Plan: 15th Actuarial Report.* Ottawa: Office of the Superintendent of Financial Institutions Canada. http://www.osfi-bsif.gc.ca/osfi/index_e.aspx?DetailID=499. (Accessed February 15, 2007.)

———. 1997. *Canada Pension Plan: 16th Actuarial Report.* Ottawa: Office of the Superintendent of Financial Institutions Canada. http://www.osfi-bsif.gc.ca/osfi/index_e. aspx?DetailID=499. (Accessed February 15, 2007.)

———. 2002. *Canada Pension Plan: 19th Actuarial Report.* Ottawa: Office of the Superintendent of Financial Institutions Canada. http://www.osfi-bsif.gc.ca/osfi/index_e. aspx?DetailID=499. (Accessed February 15, 2007.)

———. 2003. *Canada Pension Plan: 20th Actuarial Report.* Ottawa: Office of the Superintendent of Financial Institutions Canada. http://www.osfi-bsif.gc.ca/osfi/index_e. aspx?DetailID=499. (Accessed February 15, 2007.)

———. 2004. *Canada Pension Plan: 21st Actuarial Report.* Ottawa: Office of the Superintendent of Financial Institutions Canada. http://www.osfi-bsif.gc.ca/osfi/index_e. aspx?DetailID=499. (Accessed February 15, 2007.)

———. 2005. *Old Age Security: 7th Actuarial Report.* Ottawa: Office of the Superintendent of Financial Institutions Canada. http://www.osfi-bsif.gc.ca/app/DocRepository/1/eng/reports/oca/oas7_e.pdf. (Accessed February 15, 2007.)

U.S. Social Security Administration. 2005a. *2005 OASDI Trustees Report: Table VI.F5. Ratio of OASDI Taxable Payroll to GDP, Calendar Years 2005–80.* Washington, DC: U.S. Social Security Administration. http://www.ssa.gov/OACT/TR/TR05/VI_OASDHI_GDP.html#wp126788. (Accessed February 15, 2007.)

———. 2005b. *Annual Report of the Supplemental Security Income Program.* Washington, DC: U.S. Social Security Administration.

Parameters of the Canadian Public Pension and Old Age Security Systems

I f more information is required, please refer to Government of Canada (2006a, c). Note that tables do not provide information on the Québec Pension Plan; please refer to Government of Québec (2006).

Canada Pension Plan

The Canada Pension Plan (CPP) is a compulsory and contributory social insurance program designed to provide a measure of protection to workers and their families against loss of earnings due to retirement, disability, or death.

Retirement Pensions

A retirement pension is payable to each contributor at age 60 or older. The monthly amount is equal to 25 percent of the contributor's average monthly pensionable earnings during the contributory period. For retirement pensions taken before the "normal" retirement age of 65, benefits are reduced by 0.5 percent for each month that the recipient is under 65 years old. The maximum reduction is 30 percent for people retiring at age 60. In December 2005, the average monthly benefit paid was C$463.67 (Government of Canada 2006d).

Table A1.1. Key Canada Pension Plan Statistics, 2005–2006

Number of contributors	11.9 million
Amount of contributions (C$)	30.2 billion
Amount of benefits (C$)	24.9 billion
Benefits as a percentage of gross domestic product (2005)	1.8

Sources: Government of Canada (2006a); Office of the Superintendent (2003, 2004).

Disability Pensions

The disability benefit includes a flat-rate portion and an amount equal to 75 percent of the earned retirement pension. In December 2005, the average monthly benefit paid was C$758.33 (Government of Canada 2006d).

Survivor Benefits

Survivor benefits are payable to the spouse or common-law partner of a deceased contributor. For a beneficiary younger than 65, the benefit consists of a flat-rate portion and an amount equal to 37.5 percent of the deceased contributor's earned retirement pension. For beneficiaries 65 and older, the benefit is equal to 60 percent of the retirement pension granted to the deceased contributor. A beneficiary between the ages of 35 and 45 who is not disabled or who has no dependent children receives reduced

Table A1.2. Canada Pension Plan Contribution Rates and Indexation

	Rate	Indexation
Contribution rate (% of earnings)		
Employee/employer	4.95	No planned increases
Self-employed	9.90	No planned increases
Maximum contribution (2006, C$)		
Employee/employer	1,910.70	Indexed to wages
Self-employed	3,821.40	Indexed to wages
Year's basic exemption (C$)	3,500.00	Frozen
Year's maximum pensionable earnings (C$)	42,100.00	Indexed to wages

Source: Government of Canada (2006a).

benefits. In December 2005, the average monthly benefit was C$300.88 (Government of Canada 2006d).

Children's Benefits

Each child of a disabled or deceased contributor is entitled to a benefit, as long as the child is younger than 18 or is between the ages of 18 and 25 and attending school full time.

Death Benefits

A death benefit is a one-time payment to the estate of a contributor. The benefit is six times the monthly retirement pension granted to the deceased contributor, or C$2,500, whichever is less.

Table A1.3. Canada Pension Plan Benefits, Recipients, and Monthly Expenditures

	2006	October 2005	
Benefit	Maximum monthly benefit (C$)	Number of beneficiaries	Total expenditures (C$, millions)
Retirement (at age 65)	844.58	3,173,063	1,470.1
Disability	1,031.05	296,518	223.7
Survivor			
Younger than 65	471.85	233,478	79.4
65 and older	506.75	729,848	202.1
Children's			
Disabled contributor	200.47	79,903	15.7
Deceased contributor	200.47	72,597	14.2
Death[a]	2,500.00	9,461	20.9
Total	n.a.	4,594,868	2,026.1

Source: Government of Canada (2006a).

a. The death benefit is a one-time lump-sum payment.

n.a. = not applicable

Indexation of Benefits

Pensions and benefits are indexed annually based on the consumer price index for Canada. The rate of indexation for 2006 was 2.3 percent.

CPP Investment Board Assets

As of December 2005, total assets under the management of the CPP Investment Board were valued at C$92.5 billion. Assets consisted of publicly traded stocks (56.6 percent), government bonds (29.7 percent), real return assets (8.4 percent), private equities (4.3 percent), and cash and money market securities (1.0 percent), and included both foreign and domestic assets (Canada Pension Plan Investment Board 2006).

Old Age Security

The Old Age Security program is one of the cornerstones of Canada's retirement income system. Together the basic Old Age Security (OAS) pension and its Guaranteed Income Supplement (GIS) and Allowance components account for 24 percent of Government of Canada transfers to persons and other levels of government (Government of Canada 2005). This program is the largest social program delivered by the federal government.

Current Program

The vast majority of Canada's 4.2 million seniors (age 65 and older) are each entitled to just over C$5,800 (in 2006) in OAS yearly, with an estimated 5 to 6 percent paying back some (or all) of their benefits because their yearly income is above the threshold for benefit reduction (C$62,144 in 2006). Approximately 36 percent of Canadian seniors receive additional support through the GIS, which is targeted specifically at low-income seniors. In addition, the Allowance provides benefits to survivors of pensioners or spouses of pensioners, age 60 to 64. For 2005–2006, total forecast expenditures for the OAS are C$23,044 million; for the GIS, C$6,221 million; and for the Allowance, C$451 million (for a combined estimate of 2.2 percent of gross domestic product) (Government of Canada 2006c; Office of the Superintendent 2005).

Expected Increases

Given the size and importance of the Old Age Security program, it is reviewed every three years by the Office of the Chief Actuary. The resulting actuarial report forecasts future expenditures to ensure appropriate federal government budget planning. The actuarial report as of December 31, 2003, stated that the number of recipients is expected to more than double by 2030 to 8.9 million, due partly to the aging population. This is expected to raise total expenditures to C$37 billion in 2010 and C$110 billion, or 3.2 percent of gross domestic product, in 2030 (in current dollars) (Office of the Superintendent 2005).

Eligibility Conditions

OAS

To qualify for full or partial OAS pension benefits, a person must be 65 years old and either a Canadian citizen or a legal resident of Canada. Full benefits are payable to an individual who has lived in Canada for a total of at least 40 years after reaching age 18. A person who has lived in Canada for a minimum of 10 years after age 18 can receive one-fortieth of the full pension for each year lived in Canada after age 18.

GIS

To qualify for the GIS, an individual must receive the OAS and have an income below a certain threshold (see table A1.4).

Allowance

To qualify for the Allowance, an individual must be age 60 to 64, meet the same residential requirements as for the OAS, and be the spouse, common-law partner, or survivor of an OAS pensioner. Once Allowance recipients reach 65, they become eligible for OAS and GIS.

Benefit Payments

OAS

OAS is paid monthly and is independent of marital status. Pensioners with individual income over a threshold (C$62,144 in 2006) repay benefits at a rate of 15 percent of income above the threshold.

Table A1.4. Benefits Granted by the Old Age Security Program

Benefit	January–March 2006		October 2005	
	Maximum rate (C$)	Income cut-off[a] (C$)	Number of beneficiaries	Amount paid (C$, millions)
Old Age Security	484.63	n.a.	4,193,190	1,915.0
Guaranteed Income Supplement				
Single	593.97	14,256	933,028	363.2
Spouse/Common-law partner of				
A nonpensioner	593.97	34,368	80,524	31.2
A pensioner	389.67	18,720	447,670	107.1
An Allowance recipient	389.67	34,368	62,388	19.7
Allowance				
Regular	874.30	26,496	62,382	20.8
Survivor	967.24	19,368	29,823	15.7

Source: Government of Canada (2006c).

a. Income cut-off excludes OAS. If OAS were included, the income cut-off would be higher by C$5,816 and C$11,631 for singles and couples (both pensioners), respectively.

n.a. = not applicable

GIS

Benefits are based on family income (excluding OAS) and marital status. The maximum monthly supplement is reduced by 50 percent for every dollar of income (other than OAS) for singles and by 25 percent per person for couples.

Indexation of Benefits

All benefits payable under the Old Age Security Act are indexed quarterly to the consumer price index.

Stuart Butler

Réal Bouchard's chapter has brought back a memory of one of my trips to Canada about 15 years ago, to speak on Social Security. As I went through customs in the Toronto airport with a package of material for handouts, the officer said, "What is this? Is this something you were bringing to sell in Canada?" And I said, no, these are economics papers that I am going to hand out.

He wrote down, "contents: economics papers; value: zero." So I think we should maintain perspective when giving advice or commentary on another country's policy issues.

Looking at other countries' public pension reforms can be instructive. But if we are to learn from them, we have to think carefully about the conditions that prevailed at the time of a change, and whether they are relevant to the United States. That is to say, we must think about whether the policies can cross the border, and if they were to cross the border, how they would be implemented.

First of all, Bouchard emphasizes strongly that timing was critical to Canada's reforms. A real shock was provided by the 1995 report that the Canada Pension Plan was in dire financial shape. More generally, economic conditions deteriorated (Bouchard mentions that the public sector's total debt had reached 70 percent of gross domestic product), and that shook Canadians into thinking about their system's problems in a fundamentally different way.

In the United States, we have not experienced such debt since 1950. There is anxiety about the solvency of our Social Security system, but we have not seen anxiety similar to Canada's since the early 1980s, when Social Security checks were in danger of being a few weeks or months late. So the sense of crisis that was a necessary condition for the Canadian reforms is certainly not evident in the U.S. today, and certainly wasn't evident in the 1990s either, when Canada was able to reform its pension system.

Today, those of us who are trying to get Americans to think hard about the federal government's huge unfunded liabilities have an uphill struggle to convince people that there is a problem. Interest rates are low, the economy seems to be going well, and so on. It is hard to imagine the United States facing the kind of conditions that facilitated the Canadian reforms in the foreseeable future, or at least in the short-term future.

Bouchard also emphasized that broad public consultation regarding options for reform was critically important, and I think that is a valuable lesson. And as he pointed out, Canadians were forced to think about some fundamental principles affecting their system: for example, should workers make higher contributions to sustain their system without passing new debt to the next generation?

We are not yet willing to accept or even honestly debate such notions here in the United States. Certainly, raising contribution levels to sustain the Social Security system and to ward off debt to future generations was not thoroughly debated in the discussion of reform last year.

Compare the public discussion on Social Security in the U.S. during President Bill Clinton's administration with more recent public discussion. President Clinton held a number of town hall meetings and other public discussions, a positive way to engage the country in thinking about the future of the Social Security system.

Unfortunately, that momentum eroded toward the end of the Clinton administration. The discussion morphed into the notion of using the unified budget surplus to finance general revenue contributions to Social Security. It was a typically American magic-bullet approach that allowed us to avoid thinking about real structural changes to the system. The desire was to find a quick answer, and some of that same desire spilled over into last year's debate.

President George W. Bush's discussion with the American people was very different from Canada's discussion or President Clinton's. Indeed, President Bush hardly had a discussion at all. He was trying to sell a particular proposal—partial privatization of Social Security—to the American people without thoroughly testing and molding public opinion. The administration can be faulted for that, but I think we should also recognize that conditions were different in the United States than in Canada: no immediate crisis affected either the long-term future of Social Security or the government's budget. Therefore, the kind of rethinking that we saw in Canada was not necessary.

Another major difference between Canada and the United States is that Canadians were much more willing to allow government to invest public funds in the private marketplace than Social Security reformers have been in the United States. Remember that Canada's motto is "peace, order, and good government," whereas ours is "life, liberty, and the pursuit of happiness." We tend to be more skeptical of government than the Canadians, and perhaps for good reasons.

The main reason for investing in the private market is to get better returns, to improve the pension system's long-term viability. In the United States, of course, reformers attempted to invest in the private market through personal accounts, but that proposal was rejected as it was in Canada. But any proposal for government investment of Social Security funds would likely be rejected in the United States. We show a lot more concern here about the impact on asset control and the economy than we saw in the debate in Canada. Alan Greenspan raised two particular concerns relevant here: one economic or technical, and one political.

The technical concern was that national savings are unlikely to show a net increase as a result of government investment. Privatization may only be a zero-sum game. The Social Security trust fund may simply switch its portfolio from holding government bonds to holding private securities, while private investors would hold more of the former and less of the latter. This would, in no way, increase the economy's capacity to sustain the pension system.

And the second, political concern—and I agree with Greenspan on this—stressed that while some other countries may be able to create a public investment board independent of political influence, it is hard to imagine accomplishing this in the United States. And if the board is not truly independent, it could seriously jeopardize the economy and financial markets.[1]

Our experience with the public investment of state pension programs in the United States has not been reassuring. We see many mistakes and much inefficiency. Often, investments are used to spur local economic development by investing in favored companies or favored economic projects, rather than to maximize returns. Such policies would be of great concern to the United States federal government. So even if public investment is shown to work well in Canada, it just would not be accepted across the border.

Other elements of the Canadian reform would not easily cross the border today. Americans would not stomach the sharp rise in contribution tax rates required as part of the Canadian reform. For instance, to the extent that higher contribution levels were considered in the United States, the increase was more about raising the income ceiling for contributions than raising tax rates for people already paying them. In the end, Americans were not willing to contemplate either raising taxes or reducing benefits. Certainly, they would not have accepted the reductions in disability benefits enacted in Canada or even the mild reductions in pension benefits.

So in conclusion, it is depressing but realistic to note that the conditions that enabled reform in Canada are not present in the United States and may not be for some time to come. Indeed, they may never emerge here given the aging of the baby boom generation and their immense political power. Also, timing is everything—even if the right conditions emerge in the United States, the timing is unlikely to be as propitious as it was in Canada.

And last, I would point to the great irony of what has happened in the United States. The left is applauding the failure of a reform that included partial privatization. The real fear now, from the left's point of view, should instead be a continuous expansion of personal accounts in the purely tax-advantaged area—401(k)s, IRAs, and so on—such that over the years people become less and less concerned about the underlying Social Security system. That, in turn, may reduce the political support for Social Security and cause it to erode—the worst nightmare of AARP and other supporters of the traditional system. While on the one hand personal accounts and partial privatization were resoundingly rejected, those who oppose privatization may in fact get a more complete version of it.

NOTE

1. Testimony by Alan Greenspan, House Energy and Commerce Committee, Subcommittee on Finance and Hazardous Materials, March 3, 1999. http://www.federalreserve.gov/BOARDDOCS/Testimony/1999/19990303.htm. (Accessed February 14, 2007.)

James C. Capretta

Réal Bouchard's chapter and the others in this volume are useful and thought provoking because examining other countries' public pension systems can provide insights into the United States' current situation. This allows us to discuss Social Security a little bit differently. Foreign experience can provide either a pessimistic or optimistic view of the world, depending on how we look at it.

The Canadians have a defined benefit pension plan and somewhat worse population aging than in the United States. The Canadian Pension Plan was in trouble and would have required the tax rate on wages to be raised to 14 percent to keep the system financially viable. Their reforms brought the necessary tax rate down to 9.9 percent.

One aspect of Canada's demographic situation that Bouchard did not emphasize involves the role of immigration. Barbara Boyle Torrey and Nicholas Eberstadt in "The Northern America Fertility Divide" (2005) pointed out that the Canadian fertility rate is much lower than the American. It has been lower for at least a decade now and is projected to continue to be lower in the long term.

To some extent, Canadians compensate for their low fertility rate with a slightly higher net immigration rate. If we assume a zero immigration rate for the United States, the working-age population would decline by about 2 percent between now and 2050. If the same assumption were made for Canada, the decline would be about 25 percent. However, Canada's actual assumption of substantial immigration is a factor in making sure their system can be sustained with a tax rate as modest as 9.9 percent. For countries with even lower fertility rates than Canada's, how much reliance are they placing on immigration to help maintain their public pension systems? Over a long period, immigration can make a big difference to the size of the taxpaying labor force.

A second aspect of the Canadian reform is touched on only briefly in the chapter: ensuring that the reform will be stable in the long run by introducing an automatic mechanism for freezing benefits and raising taxes if the system runs into financial problems. Other countries, such as Sweden, Japan, and Germany, also have provisions in place now that will reduce benefit growth automatically if they encounter adverse demographic or economic developments.

Canada's automatic mechanism does not have quite as many teeth as do other countries'. The Canadian cabinet can vitiate the automatic benefit freeze and tax increases with a direct order. They do not need to go to the parliament for permission.

I wouldn't bet that the automatic changes would ever go into effect. There would be strong political pressures to suspend the automatic adjustments. Nonetheless, the automatic mechanism does create a political obligation to deal with adverse developments more directly. Sweden, Germany, and Japan have even stronger automatic provisions that may be more sustainable than Canada's.

So much of our discussion here focuses solely on retirement. But I think Canada's emphasis on disability benefits in their 1997 reform is also important. The reform successfully curbed escalating costs in their disability program, a problem that will have to be addressed eventually in the United States. While our retirement system's problems are solvable and readily understood in terms of their benefit implications, the disability side is more difficult to fix, as the problem essentially revolves around the definition of disability. Much more work will need to be done before the disability program can be reformed with broad support.

In one sense, the United States is not that different from Canada. We also raised our payroll tax rates substantially, in 1977 and 1983, to partially prefund Social Security. We are still running big surpluses.

The question is whether we follow the Canadian example and improve Social Security's financial status through private investment of those surplus funds. Do we want those higher private rates of return inside our government, or outside of the government in the form of individual accounts?

Most macroeconomic analyses will say, if more of the rate of return remains inside the government, a little less will probably be outside. So the choice may not make much difference economically, but it could make a big difference politically. As Stuart Butler noted in his commentary, isolating investment decisions from crass political motives might be more difficult in the United States. Because of such political concerns, the United States has chosen to do a little bit of prefunding while forgoing the opportunity to increase Social Security's returns with a private investment strategy.

REFERENCE

Torrey, Barbara Boyle, and Nicholas Eberstadt. 2005. "The Northern America Fertility Divide." *Policy Review* August–September (132): 39–55.

2

Sweden

Agneta Kruse and Edward Palmer

Sweden's public expenditures on pensions are projected to be among the lowest in Europe from 2030 to 2050, and are expected to remain around 11 percent of gross domestic product (GDP) for the next half century (table 2.1). This stability, in spite of an aging population, is due to Sweden's new pension system.

Reform of Sweden's old-age pension system was legislated by its parliament in 1994 and launched in 1999. The new design makes the system robust to economic and demographic changes and imposes transparency and financial discipline on the political machinery governing its distributive features. This financial stability stems from several attributes.

First, the pension's earnings-related component is based on defined contributions—combining a nonfinancial (i.e., notional) defined contribution (NDC) scheme with a financial defined contribution (FDC) scheme. After the reform, the earnings-related component became financially self-contained and hence, autonomous from the central government budget.

Second, the NDC scheme is indexed by the growth of the covered wage per capita, which means that the system adjusts to economic change. An autonomous adjustment mechanism maintains long-term balance between system assets and liabilities.

Third is the feature required to maintain internal balance in both the NDC and FDC schemes: financing of the distributional components

35

Table 2.1. Pension Expenditure Projections for European Countries (percent of gross domestic product)

	2004	2030	2050
Portugal	11.1	16.0	20.8
Spain	8.6	11.8	15.7
Belgium	10.4	14.7	15.5
France	12.8	14.3	14.8
Italy	14.2	15.0	14.7
Finland	10.7	14.0	13.7
Germany	11.4	12.3	13.1
Denmark	9.5	12.8	12.8
Austria	13.4	14.0	12.2
Sweden	10.6	11.1	11.2
Netherlands	7.7	10.7	11.2
Ireland	4.7	7.9	11.1
UK	6.6	7.9	8.6

Source: Economic Policy Committee and the European Commission (2006).

(notably the guarantee pension, noncontributory rights, and rights received during publicly insured periods of sickness, unemployment, and disability) is now separated from the old-age pension system and covered by the government budget.

Finally, whereas previously (as in other national social security systems) disability and survivor benefits were a part of the overall pension system, these as well are now separate from the old-age system and are covered by general budget revenues.

The Previous Swedish Pension System

In the latter half of the 1980s, a lengthy investigation by Sweden's Pension Commission showed the system to be financially unsustainable (see the projected expenditures in table 2.2). The old system was a public defined benefit system consisting of two parts: a basic flat-rate benefit (the *folkpension*) and an earnings-related supplementary benefit (the *ATP*). A rather large buffer fund, with assets equal to about five years of payments at the time of the reform, was administered outside the state budget.

There were several sources of instability inherent in the old system. First, new workers were gradually postponing their entry into the labor market, a trend that has continued to date. All other things being equal, this has reduced labor force participation.

Second, although at the end of the 1990s Swedes worked to an older age than workers in most countries (see, for example, Palme and Svensson 1999 and Palmer 1999), without a mechanism to increase the pensionable age—or encourage younger workers to enter the labor force earlier—their years of contributions would decline. Concurrently, life expectancy from age 60 has increased by about four years since as recently as 1960, and projections indicate a continued trend upward. Also in the early 1990s, the labor force participation of women born in the 1940s and later was expected to match that of men. However, while the trend from the 1970s has been for women to increase the number of years they participate in the labor force, men's participation was declining, with later entry and earlier exit than in the 1960s and 1970s.[1] What was already clear by then was that it would no longer be possible to count on women's increasing labor force participation to counteract men's declining age of exit.

Third, an even more important source of instability was the old system's reliance on good economic growth to hold down benefit costs relative to the wage sum, but then only at the expense of becoming a system where most workers' earnings would eventually surpass the ceiling on coverage—with the portion over the ceiling increasing with time. This meant that the earnings-related *ATP* scheme was gradually evolving into a flat-rate benefit, albeit a larger one than the already-existing *folkpension*.

Moreover, as is true of all defined benefit pay-as-you-go schemes, price indexation made system expenditures easier to finance with more growth. With high growth, as in the 1980s, the need for reform appears less urgent. With low growth, as in the 1990s (with negative growth in the first half of the decade), reform becomes urgent. This perverse relation between financial stability and growth was increasingly viewed as untenable by policy experts and politicians. The combination of real growth and the ceiling on wages reduced the cost of pensions, as the comparison of 3 percent growth to lower growth in table 2.2 illustrates. Coverage was also being eroded with real growth, given that the ceiling on pensionable earnings was only price indexed.

Also, because the *ATP* required that recipients only make 30 years of contributions to receive a full benefit, and the benefit was based on the

Table 2.2. Projected Swedish Government Expenditures on the *ATP* and *Folkpension* (percent of the wage sum)

	Real Rate of Growth (percent)			
	0	1	2	3
1995	19.8	19.8	19.8	19.8
2025	35.6	27.3	21.2	16.2
2050	36.0	24.0	15.2	9.1

Source: Working Group on Pensions (1994).

Notes: ATP was the earnings-related, supplementary portion of the benefit from Sweden's previous old-age pension system; the *folkpension* was the flat-rate portion granted to all pensioners.

15 best years of earnings and contributions, its defined benefit design gave rise to a perverse income redistribution effect. Empirical studies (e.g., Ståhlberg 1995) confirmed that the system transferred resources from workers with relatively low incomes throughout their lives (e.g., blue-collar workers) to workers whose incomes rose relatively steeply over their careers (e.g., professionals).

The New Swedish Pension System

Sweden's new public pension system consists of three parts, an NDC component (the *inkomstpension*), an FDC component (the *premiepension*), and a guaranteed benefit level (the guarantee pension).[2,3] The first two are defined contribution schemes with the contributions set at 16 percent and 2.5 percent of earnings, respectively. The guarantee pension is a defined benefit scheme, where the benefit is means tested against an individual's combined NDC and FDC pensions. The guarantee pension is financed by general taxation from the central government budget.

The Notional Defined Contribution Scheme

The notional defined contribution (NDC) scheme is a defined contribution, pay-as-you-go scheme.[4] Each person has a notional account in which the contributions accrue. Contributions are used to pay outgoing benefits to contemporary pensioners. The account is indexed to the country's economic growth (i.e., to the change in average covered wages). Contributions are paid on all earnings from all years of labor force participation.[5] Each year, the notional account increases with new contributions and the rate of return. The accounts are also accredited with inheritance gains from the notional accounts of deceased persons belonging to the same cohort.[6] Benefits from unemployment insurance, sickness and disability insurance, and parental leave are treated as income; contributions on this income are paid into the individual's account. These contributions are financed from their respective insurance (i.e., from the central government budget; see Pensions and the Budget Process below). Also, pension credits are given for some activities outside the labor market: military service, higher education, and raising children. These, too, are financed from the central government budget.

The NDC benefit is a yearly payment until death, determined by dividing pension wealth by an annuity divisor calculated by life expectancy at the time of retirement, and an imputed real rate of return (1.6 percent) during the expected life of the annuity.[7] Benefits are price indexed and adjusted further for deviations (positive and negative) in the real rate of growth of the average covered wage.

Using an annuity divisor based on life expectancy at retirement makes the pension system (almost) robust to increases in longevity, thus (almost) eliminating the effect of increasing longevity on pension costs. It also means that the higher the life expectancy, the lower the pension benefit, all other things being equal. This can, of course, be compensated for by working longer (table 2.3).

In a defined contribution scheme, liabilities cannot exceed assets. In the Swedish NDC scheme, an automatic balancing mechanism (ABM) is applied to adjust workers' accounts and pensioners' benefits with an index based on the deviation of liabilities from assets (Palmer 2006; Settergren 2001).

How can the need for balancing arise? First, the index chosen for the Swedish system, which is based on average covered wage growth, does not reflect changes in the covered labor force. Specifically, a declining labor force constitutes a potential source of imbalance to be rectified by the ABM. Second, life expectancy will likely be greater than the value used in the annuity divisor, which is based on current cross-sectional data rather than a cohort projection. Third, changes in the stream of contributions and payments can affect the outcome (Settergren and Mikula 2006).

Table 2.3. Average Life Expectancy and Retirement Age, and Their Effect on Swedish Pension Benefits

Year cohort born	Year cohort reaches 65	Projected annuity divisor at 65	Effect of life expectancy on pension at 65 (%)	Retirement age to neutralize life-expectancy effect	Resulting estimated length of retirement
1940	2005	15.7	n.a.	65 years	18 years, 6 months
1950	2015	16.4	- 4	65 years, 8 months	18 years, 7 months
1960	2025	17.0	- 8	66 years, 2 months	19 years, 1 month
1970	2035	17.5	- 10	66 years, 7 months	19 years, 4 months
1980	2045	17.9	- 12	67 years	19 years, 6 months
1990	2055	18.1	- 14	67 years, 2 months	19 years, 10 months

Source: Swedish National Social Insurance Board (2005).

n.a. = not applicable

Finally, small technical problems will always arise because indices are based on historical average data.

The NDC scheme inherited a large buffer fund from the old system, which had been built up over three decades as an economic and demographic buffer for the old *ATP* scheme. The Swedish reform began, thus, with a stock of financial assets that would eventually mitigate the cost pressure baby-boomer retirements put on the system. A demographic or economic development negative to the pension system can be offset, thus, by a development positive to the buffer fund. Note also that, all other things being equal, a lower rate of return on the buffer fund increases the probability that the balancing mechanism will be activated—and vice versa.

The ABM is triggered when any of these situations causes system assets to fall short of liabilities. The index, both on the notional accounts and on the benefits being paid, is reduced by the ABM whenever the balance ratio is less than 1.[8] If the mechanism is triggered, accounts can undergo positive indexation until the index has gone back to its original trajectory (figure 2.1).

The Swedish Social Insurance Agency has recently published calculations for three scenarios: a base scenario, an optimistic scenario, and a pessimistic scenario.

Figure 2.1. The Automatic Balance Mechanism in the Swedish
Pension System

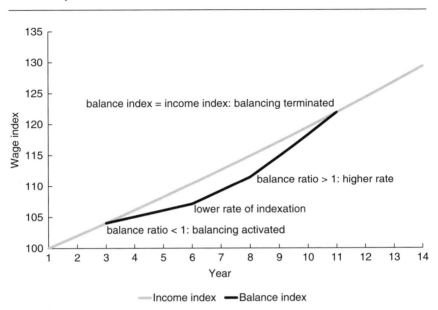

Source: Swedish National Social Insurance Board (2005).

In the base scenario, the balance ratio remains close to 1 for the next 15 years, with balancing activated in a few brief periods. After 2020 the financial position of the system strengthens. In the optimistic scenario, the consolidation ratio of the system increases for almost the entire period. By 2050, assets of the system exceed the pension liability by almost 20 percent. In the pessimistic scenario, the balance ratio drops below 1.0 in 2008; consequently, balancing is activated. (Swedish National Social Insurance Board 2005, 43)

To conclude, the NDC design makes the system robust to economic and demographic strains. Further, the defined contribution feature, with the tight connection between contributions and benefits, does not affect individual decisions regarding work effort and unlike the old defined benefit construction, rewards all years of work. By providing an incentive to work longer, the defined contribution framework may alleviate some strain caused by the expected increase in the ratio of pensioners to workers (i.e., the system dependency ratio). The calculation of yearly benefits by dividing the accumulated notional account by an annuity divisor determined by the cohort's life expectancy at retirement may also alleviate this strain. What's more, in the NDC framework, the "burden" of a longer life will not fall on the working generation, but on the workers who will enjoy it.[9]

Finally, indexing both accounts and benefits by average covered wage growth means that, in principle, the growth of pensioners' benefits follows the growth of contemporary workers' wages. In practice, however, this indexing is disguised by "front loading" NDC annuities (i.e., in calculating the annuity, 1.6 percent real growth has already been factored into the yearly payment). This in turn means that real indexation of benefits follows the growth of the real average covered wage to the extent that it deviates from 1.6 percent, not the growth of real wages per se. Because some future growth (i.e., 1.6 percent per annum) is already factored into the initial value of the annuity, the real value of benefits will not increase linearly with the real covered wage. Instead, the value will increase with the difference between the actual real growth rate and 1.6 percent—which means benefits will be adjusted downward in real terms for growth below 1.6 percent.

The Financial Defined Contribution Scheme

The financial defined contribution (FDC) scheme, like the NDC scheme, is an individual account system. However, actual money goes into the FDC account. During the accumulation phase, an account holder can choose from almost 800 funds administered by more than 80 global companies registered with the Premium Pension Authority (or PPM), a publicly managed clearinghouse. To date, the bulk of money has gone into equities. Not choosing is also an option, taken by about one-third of the covered population. These contributions go into a public default fund, administered by a public authority under the leadership of a professional board of directors.

The FDC annuity can be claimed either as unit-linked insurance or as traditional insurance. If unit-linked insurance is claimed, the annuity remains in the chosen funds and the benefit is revalued once a year, based on the December value of the fund shares. In each month of the following year, sufficient fund shares are sold to finance the pension benefit. If traditional insurance is claimed, the pension is calculated as a lifelong annuity. The money on accounts turned over to the PPM is invested by another public authority and is presently yielding a bond rate of return.

The Guarantee Pension

The guarantee pension is a narrowly means-tested benefit based solely on a pensioner's combined NDC and FDC benefits. It is a pay-as-you-go defined benefit, is price indexed, and is financed from the central government budget.

The lowest pension benefit granted in 2004 was kr6,200 if married and just below kr7,000 if unmarried. In 2004, the average monthly wage was kr23,700. The lowest pension was thus 30 percent of the average wage for an unmarried person. In the lowest-paid occupation the average monthly wage was kr16,300, which means that the lowest pension was 43 percent of that wage. Those receiving such low pensions are granted a housing supplement for up to 90 percent of their monthly housing costs.

Survivor Insurance

Before 1990, widows could get a pension from both the *folkpension* and the *ATP* scheme. To achieve gender equity, the widow's pension was abolished in 1990 for persons born in 1945 and later and was replaced by an adjustment pension, eligible to both widows and widowers. The adjustment pension is granted for a year, with continued support possible in special cases. Surviving children receive pensions until the age of 18 or, for students, until the age of 20.

The Expected Outcome

In considering outcomes for individuals from the new system, comparisons are often made between the benefits expected from the old system and the benefits expected from the new system. What is forgotten in these comparisons is that the old system was unsustainable. Piecemeal changes would have been inevitable and without them, some future generation would be facing a bankrupt pension system.

The new Swedish pension system promises no specific outcome. Newly granted benefits depend on each individual's capital balance upon retirement—notional in the NDC scheme and actual in the FDC scheme—and on the annuity divisors for each of these. To some extent, the individual can influence the outcome (for example, by working longer hours or postponing retirement). And to some extent, the outcome is influenced by external factors (for example, the rate of return on individual financial and notional accounts—generally, the former is determined by the financial market's outcome and the latter by the economy's performance).

Calculating replacement rates is a notoriously difficult business. The question is, what should benefits be compared with? Often, some measure of a final salary is used. An alternative is to compare an average benefit for all pensioners at a particular point in time with that of all wage earners—a "macro" replacement rate. A version of the latter published by the social insurance administration in Sweden (Swedish National Social Insurance Board 2004) is the ratio of an average benefit at age 65 to an average wage of all people ages 16 to 64. This replacement rate is projected to decrease from around 65 percent for those born in the first part of the 1940s to below 55 percent for those born from 1970 on (figure 2.2).

Figure 2.2 also illustrates the different parts of the Swedish system. It shows how the old *ATP* system will be phased out, with the birth cohort born in 1953 being the last one to receive benefits from both the old and the new systems. In addition, it shows the increasing importance of the FDC pension. With continued price indexation, the guarantee pension

Figure 2.2. Pension at Age 65, Compared with Income at Ages 16 to 64, by Cohort

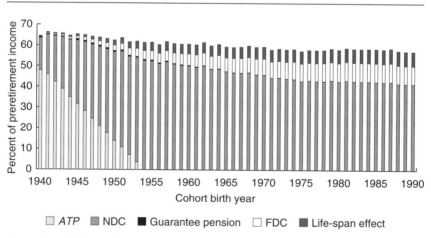

Source: Swedish National Social Insurance Board (2004, 47).

ATP = earnings-related supplementary benefit

FDC = financial defined contribution scheme

NDC = notional defined contribution scheme

becomes less and less important. It is doubtful, however, that the real value of the guarantee pension will be permitted to wither away forever. Sweden's economic history tells us that sooner or later, politicians will raise these benefits. The figure also illustrates how increases in longevity affect the pension benefit (i.e., the life-span effect).

The definition of the replacement rate used in figure 2.2 is not the most common one. Different figures are derived when the replacement rate is defined as the average pension during ages 65 to 69 in relation to average income during ages 60 to 64 (see table 2.4).

According to these calculations, cohorts born later will have lower replacement rates than those born in the 1940s. Also, lower-income groups have higher replacement rates from the public system, thanks to the guarantee pension and the ceiling on contributions. In contrast, contractual benefits are more important in high-income groups than in low-income groups (see note 3).

Ståhlberg, Kruse, and Sundén (2005) provide an estimate of the relative outcome for men and women receiving public pensions. Because the labor market behavior of women often differs from that of men, women are divided into four groups. First, the *full-career woman,* assumed to have the same labor market behavior as a man. Second, the *full-time/part-time woman* who works full-time until having children, has two children,

Table 2.4. Replacement Rate at Ages 65–69 in Relation to Average Income at Ages 60–64, by Cohort and Income Group

Cohort	Income group (percentile)	Percent of total income	Of which public pension	Contractual benefit	Private voluntary pension
1940	Below 25th	112	84	8	18
	25th–75th	74	54	10	9
	Above 75th	67	37	17	11
1950	Below 25th	87	63	12	11
	25th–75th	68	46	13	7
	Above 75th	57	27	22	7
1960	Below 25th	79	57	13	7
	25th–75th	65	44	15	6
	Above 75th	59	29	24	5

Source: Flood (2004).

alternates between parental leave and part-time work while the children are young, then returns to work full-time. Third, the *10-year woman* who works for 10 years early in life, before marriage and children.[10] Fourth, the woman who works part-time most of her working life, the *part-time woman*. For each of the profiles, estimates are made for five educational groups for newly granted benefits (table 2.5).

On average, women's benefits are lower than men's. But women's replacement rates are always at least as good as or better than full-career men's. Women also have higher rates of return on lifetime contributions than men. Men have higher earnings and therefore reach the ceiling more often than women, which gives them somewhat lower replacement rates from the mandatory public system (table 2.5).

The replacement rate for women is always at least as good or better than for a full-career man. This result is attributable in part to the use of unisex life-expectancy tables in the computation of the NDC and FDC annuities (as women generally outlive men). In addition, for women with short earnings careers, the minimum pension guarantee and the pension credits granted for child rearing help hold up replacement rates. Generally speaking, however, both men and women with low lifetime earnings, which qualify them for a guarantee benefit, will tend to have high replacement rates. This is illustrated by the substantial rates of return for 10-year women (table 2.5).

Whether these benefits and replacement rates are "sufficient" depends among other things on what the pension is supposed to buy. Consider that health care is provided by the public sector in Sweden (although with

Table 2.5. Women's Pensions as a Percentage of a Full-Career Man's Pension

	Full-career woman	Full-time/ Part-time woman	10-year woman	Part-time woman
Newly granted benefit	80–100	80[a]	35–40	60–70
Replacement rate	100–120	100–120	120–145	100–125
Rate of return	115–130	120[a]	310–400	120–130

Source: Ståhlberg, Kruse, and Sundén (2005).

Note: The first figure in the interval shows those with no upper secondary school education, the last figure, those with postgraduate education.

a. The outcome is the same for all educational groups.

a patient fee per visit, up to a ceiling) and that other old-age care is highly subsidized. In addition, what may be sufficient for couples may be less sufficient for people living on their own, usually widows, who cannot take advantage of the economies of scale inherent in two-person households.

Pensions and the Budget Process

The NDC pension scheme is designed to be autonomous from the central government budget, as is the FDC scheme by definition. Both are financed by contributions paid by employers, employees, the state, and the self-employed. These contributions do not go into the state budget, but to the NDC buffer fund and the individual financial accounts managed by the *PPM*.

Contributions on earnings are partially financed by employers and partly by employees. The split was intended to be 50/50 in the multiparty agreement preceding the first legislation in 1994, but the split has ended up at 62/38 (table 2.6).

Also, pensions not directly based on contributions on earnings are now financed from the central government budget. First is the guarantee pension, which amounted to 13.8 percent of old-age expenditures in 2004.

Table 2.6. Pension Contributions to the Swedish Notional Defined Contribution and Financial Defined Contribution Schemes, 2004 (kr, billions)

	Employer/ Self-employed	Central government	Employee/ Individual	Total
Individual earnings	107	0	65	172
Insured periods of sickness, unemployment, parental leave, etc. (transfer payments)	0	11	7	18
Disability	0	10	0	10
Noncontributory rights (e.g., child care years)	0	7	0	7
Total	107	28	72	207

Source: Swedish National Social Insurance Board (2005).

Second, payments from social insurance to individuals, such as sickness insurance, unemployment insurance, disability pensions, and parental leave compensation, are pension-qualifying income. Third are noncontributory rights for activities other than employment in the labor market: child care, higher education, and compulsory national service. Contributions for these benefits are also paid from the central government budget.

Thus, state contributions cover two kinds of pension rights, noncontributory rights and rights granted for socially insured periods of sickness, disability, unemployment, and parental leave compensated by social insurance. Individuals also pay the "employee" contribution during periods covered by public insurance for sickness, unemployment, and parental leave. Finally, the state finances all expenses for the guarantee pension, including housing supplements.

Table 2.6 shows that of a total of kr207 billion paid into the Swedish pension system in 2004, kr107 billion was paid by employers; kr28 billion, by the central government, and kr72 billion by insured individuals. Thus in 2004, 13 percent of the contributions to the NDC and FDC schemes were financed from the central government budget. Importantly, however, these contributions have been placed in the NDC reserve funds and individual financial accounts. Whether the money deposited in the NDC funds constitutes an increase in public-sector saving depends on the funds' outcome and is difficult to identify separately from other public-sector revenues. Money going into FDC accounts constitutes an increment to saving. In both cases, however, the net system effect will depend on whether individuals decrease their private saving, compared to what they would have saved without the reform.

In 2004, the state also paid about kr25 billion for guarantee benefits. Of this amount, about kr24 billion financed legacy commitments from the old system and kr1 billion financed new commitments. Those who qualify for the guarantee under the new system must have been born in 1938 or later.

Table 2.7 provides projections of the old-age pension costs for the state budget produced by the Ministry of Finance. The guarantee pension is price indexed and, to date, has not been altered since it could first be claimed in January 2002 (when pensioners shifted to the new system). In the projections to 2050, the guarantee pension was assumed to be indexed to nominal wage growth from 2010, to maintain its relative real value. The guarantee pension was about 1.3 percent of GDP in 2004, and without real indexation will decline to about 0.5 percent in 2010. After 2010, the projections assume that the state's expenditures increase at the same rate

Table 2.7. Projected Central Budget Outlays for the Guarantee Pension and Pension Credits (kr, billions)

	2010	2020	2030	2040	2050
Guarantee pension	24	40	61	94	130
Old-age pension contributions for					
Transfer payments	8	13	19	27	41
Disability pensions and pension- qualifying amounts	23	33	52	75	112
Total	55	86	132	196	283
Percent of gross domestic product	1.7	1.7	1.8	1.8	1.8

Source: Ministry of Finance, Sweden (2005).

as GDP, reflecting nominal wage—instead of price—indexation of the guarantee.

The guarantee benefit by itself is not sufficient to bring an individual with no other sources of income up to the minimum standard of living set by the National Welfare Board. To come up to this level, the individual must also claim a means-tested housing allowance, also financed from the state budget. Hence, a full picture of the Swedish model must encompass this state expenditure too. Total expenditures on old-age, disability, and survivor benefits and adjustment pensions are kr270.4 billion, or about 10.6 percent of GDP in 2004 (table 2.8).

What Made Reform Possible?

Many countries have pay-as-you-go, defined benefit pension systems, making them vulnerable to demographic changes such as aging populations. Sweden had such a system, but has reformed it in a way we claim has made it stable and robust. Reform proposals in other countries have been met with fierce resistance and large demonstrations by the "grey panthers." From a social choice perspective, such reactions are expected.[11] The question, then, is this: how was it possible to launch such a reform in Sweden when, so far, it has not been possible in other, similar countries?[12]

In 1990, a parliamentary committee produced a report on the old pension system's financial status and concluded that it was not sustainable.

Table 2.8. Total Expenditures on Old-Age, Disability, and Survivor Benefits from the Swedish Central Budget, 2004 (kr, billions)

Benefit	Expenditure (kr, billions)
Old-age pension[a]	180.0
Housing supplements to old-age pensioners	8.0
Disability pension[b]	64.0
Housing supplements to disability pensioners	3.0
Survivor benefits	15.0
Adjustment pensions	0.4
Total	270.4

Source: Swedish National Social Insurance Board (2005).

a. The guarantee pension accounts for kr25 billion of these expenditures.

b. Pension credits account for kr10 billion of these expenditures.

Maintaining the old system would require an increase in the contribution rate (if economic growth were low), or conversion to a flat-rate pension system (if economic growth were high or normal), owing to the price-indexed ceiling on pension-qualifying earnings. In addition, as was discussed above, the old system's defined benefit design gave rise to a perverse income redistribution and did not provide incentives to postpone retirement, even with increasing life expectancy. Both situations are detrimental to a pay-as-you-go system.

As it happened, in the early 1990s, Sweden experienced an economic crisis with negative economic growth three years in a row. The resulting drop of almost 10 percent in GDP and the public pension's contribution base emphasized the system's vulnerability. This made the Swedish people conscious of the necessity for structural reform and underlined its urgency. At the time, the system had a large fund amounting to about five years of current pension payments. This fund facilitated the transition, as it was, among other things, a good buffer: the contribution rate in the NDC scheme could be set as "low" as 18.5 percent to cover previous old-age benefits and ease the transition to an NDC scheme, while new NDC old-age benefits could be paid with a contribution rate of 16 percent and an FDC contribution rate of 2.5 percent. As mentioned above, disability pensions and guarantee pensions are no longer part of the old-age pension system. However, money was also transferred from the buffer fund to the central government to compensate for these "new" obligations. At the same time, the rules for the buffer fund were liberalized so that a large share of assets could be invested in the equity market at the discretion of the funds' boards, albeit following prudent rules for asset-liability management.

Politically, the reform was facilitated by forming not a large parliamentary committee, but instead a small working group consisting of representatives from the political parties in the parliament (discussed in more detail in Könberg, Palmer, and Sundén 2006). Five of the seven parties in Parliament, representing 85 percent of the votes, lined up behind the agreement. The agreed-upon transition rules made it possible to form a majority in favor of the new system. (Persons born in 1954 will be the first covered entirely by the new system. Persons born in 1953 will have 1/20 of their benefits based on the old system and 19/20 on the new system, and so on.) Also, a transition rule was constructed to guarantee that pension benefits would never fall short of those earned at the date of the reform.

With five political parties partaking in the agreement, the resulting design is a compromise, with each party winning in some aspects and losing in others. To date, the compromise has been politically stable. Of course, whether the agreement will hold in the long run is an empirical issue. An attempt to implement changes to the agreement without the consent of all five parties may lead to demands to renegotiate the whole agreement—such a risk may deter *any* government from initiating reform proposals.

NOTES

1. This trend was broken in the latter 1990s, followed by a gradual increase in the participation of both older male and older female workers.

2. For a comparison of ways to organize pension systems, see Góra and Palmer (2004).

3. There is also a fourth part, contractual benefits determined in negotiations between labor and employer confederations. There are four major negotiation sectors covering about 90 percent of the Swedish labor force. The additional contribution rate collected in conjunction with contractual benefits is approximately 3.5 to 4.5 percent. As a result of the reform, these plans began converting to a defined contribution supplement for pensions based on earnings under the ceiling. These systems are, however, more important for high-income earners, since they replace 60 to 65 percent of the income above the ceiling in the social insurance system, still through a defined benefit component.

4. There are now many publications on the Swedish pension reform: for example, Palmer (2000; 2002), and, more recently, Kruse (2005) and Könberg, Palmer, and Sundén (2006). See Palmer (2006) for a more formal account of the NDC scheme and Holzmann and Palmer (2006) for an anthology of writings on the NDC scheme.

5. Pensions are only granted for income up to a ceiling. However, contributions are levied on income above the ceiling, making the contributions above the ceiling a pure tax. This tax rate is half the contribution rate.

6. Deceased persons' pension balances and premium-pension capital are distributed to surviving persons, increasing the pension balances of all insured survivors in each birth cohort by the same percentage. In 2004, the inheritance gain factor for a selection of birth cohorts was as follows.
- 1945: 1.0046
- 1950: 1.0029
- 1960: 1.0011
- 1970: 1.0004
- 1980: 1.0004

7. Because 1.6 percent real growth has already been factored into the NDC payment (i.e., "front loaded"), the divisor is always smaller than the remaining estimated life expectancy. In 2004, the following divisors were determined for the 1944 cohort at alternate retirement ages.
- 61: 19.02
- 62: 17.44
- 63: 16.86
- 64: 16.27
- 65: 15.69

8. $BR = (CA + F) / D$, where BR is the balance ratio, CA, the contribution asset, F, the buffer fund, and D, the pension liability.

9. Thus, the annuity divisor is set when the cohort reaches 65 years of age. Changes or increases in longevity after that date are not accommodated into the annuity divisor. Instead, these changes are accommodated by the automatic balance mechanism.

10. In Sweden, this behavior is an exception. However, it shows the outcome for women who do not have their own pension (or who have a very small pension).

11. See for example Browning (1975) and Breyer and Craig (1997) for theoretical and empirical evidence. See also Kruse (2005) for a discussion of the Swedish reform from a social choice perspective.

12. Since the Swedish reform, there have been reforms in other countries. Poland and Latvia are two examples, both having had transition economies with broken-down pension systems.

REFERENCES

Breyer, Friedrich, and Ben Craig. 1997. "Voting on Social Security: Evidence from OECD Countries." *European Journal of Political Economy* 16(32): 7–50.

Browning, Edgar. 1975. "Why the Social Insurance Budget is Too Large in a Democracy." *Economic Inquiry* 13: 373–88.

Economic Policy Committee and the European Commission. 2006. *The Impact of Aging on Public Expenditure.* Special Report 1/2006. Brussels: Directorate-General for Economic and Financial Affairs, European Union.

Flood, Lennart. 2004. "Vilka pensioner får framtidens pensionärer?" *Ekonomisk Debatt* 3: 16–30.

Góra, Marek, and Edward Palmer. 2004. "Shifting Perspectives in Pensions." IZA Discussion Paper 1369. Warsaw: Warsaw School of Economics, Institute for the Study of Labor (IZA).

Holzmann, Robert, and Edward Palmer, eds. 2006. *Pension Reform: Issues and Prospects for Non-Financial Defined Contribution (NDC) Schemes.* Washington, DC: World Bank.

Könberg, Bo, Edward Palmer, and Annika Sundén, 2006. "The NDC Reform in Sweden: The 1994 Legislation to the Present." In *Pension Reform: Issues and Prospects for Non-Financial Defined Contribution (NDC) Schemes,* edited by Robert Holzmann and Edward Palmer (449–66). Washington, DC: World Bank.

Kruse, Agneta. 2005. "Political Economy and Pensions in Ageing Societies: A Note on How an 'Impossible' Reform Was Implemented in Sweden." Working Paper 2005:35. Lund, Sweden: Department of Economics, Lund University.

Ministry of Finance, Sweden. 2005. "Update of Sweden's Convergence Programme." Stockholm: Ministry of Finance.

Palme, Mårten, and Ingemar Svensson. 1999. "Social Security, Occupational Pensions and Retirement in Sweden." In *Social Security and Retirement around the World,* edited by Jonathan Gruber and David A. Wise (355–402). National Bureau of Economic Research Conference Report. Chicago and London: University of Chicago Press.

Palmer, Edward. 1999. "Exit from the Labor Force of Older Workers: Can the NDC Pension System Help?" *The Geneva Papers on Risk and Insurance* 24: 461–72, October.

———. 2000. "The Swedish Pension Reform: Framework and Issues." Social Protection Discussion Paper 12. Washington, DC: World Bank.

———. 2002. "Swedish Pension Reform: How Did It Evolve and What Does It Mean for the Future?" In *Coping with the Pension Crisis: Where Does Europe Stand?* edited by Martin Feldstein and Horst Siebert (171–205). Chicago: University of Chicago Press.

———. 2006. "What is NDC?" In *Pension Reform: Issues and Prospects for Non-Financial Defined Contribution (NDC) Schemes,* edited by Robert Holzmann and Edward Palmer (17–34).Washington, DC: World Bank.

Settergren, Ole. 2001. "The Automatic Balance Mechanism of the Swedish Pension System: A Non-Technical Introduction." *Wirtschaftspolitishe Blatter* 4: 339–49.

Settergren, Ole, and Boguslaw D. Mikula. 2006. "The Rate of Return of Pay-As-You-Go Pension Systems: A More Exact Consumption-Loan Model of Interest." In *Pension Reform: Issues and Prospects for Non-Financial Defined Contribution (NDC) Schemes,* edited by Robert Holzmann and Edward Palmer (117–42). Washington, DC: World Bank.

Ståhlberg, Ann-Charlotte. 1995. "Women's Pensions in Sweden." *Scandinavian Journal of Social Welfare* 4: 19–27.

Ståhlberg, Ann-Charlotte, Agneta Kruse, and Annika Sundén. 2005. "Pension Design and Gender." *European Journal of Social Security* 7(1): 57–79.

Swedish National Social Insurance Board. 2004. *The Swedish Pension System Annual Report 2003.* Stockholm: National Social Insurance Board.

———. 2005. *The Swedish Pension System Annual Report 2004.* Stockholm: National Social Insurance Board.

Working Group on Pensions. 1994. "Reformerat pensionssystem. Kostnader och individeffekter." *Betänkande av Pensionsarbetsgruppen. Bilaga A.* Official Publication 21. Stockholm: Swedish Government Official Publications.

Estelle James

The Swedish public pension system is very clever and it is very generous. Every time I read about it, I learn something that makes me realize it is even more clever and generous than I thought previously. It also contains several automatic stabilizers of interest to Americans. These automatically reduce benefit growth but push an uncertain portion of rising costs into the government's budget, and this portion is not automatically stabilized. Also, the U.S. has a very different system from Sweden, and that limits the degree to which we could simply adapt their automatic stabilizers here. In particular, our benefits are much lower than the starting point in Sweden, and we seem to have trouble controlling our government deficits.

The Swedish system consists of a large notional defined contribution plan (NDC) and a small funded defined contribution plan. The NDC represents an imaginative innovation that Sweden gave to the world for better or for worse. It has its good points and its bad points.

Let me briefly define the NDC and describe how it works. It is clever in that it offers the advantages of a close link between benefits and contributions, as in any defined contribution plan, without the transition costs of shifting to a funded system. Transition costs are always the hang-up when we talk about shifting from a pay-as-you-go system to a funded system. The NDC avoids that problem because it remains pay-as-you-go. Basically, contributions are recorded in an individual account and earn a notional interest rate equal to the average rate of wage growth. At retirement, all contributions and notional interest earnings are added. This notional accumulation, divided by an annuity factor that depends primarily on cohort life expectancy, is the pension.

But *notional* means that there is no real money in the account. Nothing is invested. Nothing is saved. The money paid in is used to pay benefits to current retirees, as in any pay-as-you-go plan. Hence the close benefit-contribution link is achieved without the transition costs of a shift to a funded system. Therefore, notional accounts have proved tempting to some countries that have large implicit pension debts. Transitioning to a new social security system would incur huge costs in such countries, and notional accounts yield some of the benefits of a defined contribution plan without transition costs.

Of course, there is always a price to pay. And the price of the NDC is retaining a pay-as-you-go system, with its low implicit rate of return. The system's financial sustainability will be affected by population aging. National saving will not increase. The NDC, also, is not redistributive in any way. That is one way that it differs from our defined benefit system—it strictly links benefits and contributions. But redistribution is achieved in other ways, in particular with a generous minimum pension. And financial sustainability is also achieved in other ways that I discuss below.

But first, let me lay out the different elements of benefits, their generosity, and how much they might cost. The Swedish pension's replacement rate is now estimated to be about 65 percent. But it's expected to fall to about 55 percent in the future because of the 1999 shift to the NDC, which gives a low rate of implicit interest and explicitly adjusts the benefit downward as life expectancy increases. Of the 55 percent replacement rate, about two-thirds will come from the NDC and one-third from the funded defined contribution. (The funded defined contribution is expected to play a larger and larger relative role as the NDC declines.) In addition to the average replacement rate, there is a minimum pension, which is 30 to 40 percent of the average wage. The minimum pension is formally price indexed, which means that it will fall as a proportion of the average wage over time. However, I appreciate the authors' honesty in pointing out that this violates Swedish political culture, and the pension will likely be linked to wages over time, thereby increasing total costs.

I have written a lot about Chile.[1] Their minimum pension is also formally price indexed, but discretionary increases have moved it up with wages over time. So we should always keep this political dynamic in mind when we talk about price indexation versus wage indexation: the political power of retirees may lead toward wage indexation, even if that wasn't intended initially. If a minimum pension is price indexed, its cost will decline relative to wages over time, but if it is wage indexed, its costs will keep up with wage growth. Sweden's minimum pension is financed from the state budget, not by earmarked contributions, so when we talk about financial sustainability of the system, we are not including the cost of the minimum pension. In addition, recipients of the minimum pension get a housing supplement that pays 90 percent of their rent. In this country, that would be a huge addition to the average Social Security benefit, let alone some minimum. Just to compare the generosity of the Swedish system to the American—the minimum benefit in Sweden (including the housing supplement) is larger than our average benefit. It's important to keep that in mind when we think about applying automatic adjustment mechanisms to the U.S. Social Security system.

The generous minimum pension and housing supplement, plus the large NDC, provides a very comfortable cushion. That means that when people invest their small funded account, they can take risks. In fact, the funds are mainly invested in equities and so will probably earn a high rate of return. Those returns will provide a nice replacement rate from the funded defined contribution that will make up for some of the declines anticipated in the NDC. So the system as a whole will remain generous.

Of course, generosity is expensive. The NDC costs 16 percent of an individual's wages, up to a wage ceiling. Additionally, 8 percent is paid above the wage ceiling, without earning any benefit credits. Another 2.5 percent of wages goes into the funded defined contribution accounts. Still another 3 to 4 percent finances an almost universal occupational pension. In addition, the government budget pays for the guaranteed pension, a housing allowance, disability and survivor insurance, and pension credits for those on parental or sickness leave, those in their child-carrying years, those receiving unemployment, and so on. Expenditures from the state budget cost the equivalent of approximately 12 to 14 percent of wages, although they come out of broader general revenues. The total cost of all these pension components seems to be about 35 percent of the country's total payroll, although the amount coming from general revenues is quite uncertain.

That seems unimaginable for the U.S., and whenever I see these numbers, I think, well, the Swedes just behave differently. Americans would expect Sweden's economy to implode with these tax burdens, but their economy keeps chugging along pretty nicely. So it's a very generous plan and it's quite different, you can see, from ours.

What are the built-in stabilizers in this system? First is the annuity factor. The notional accumulation is turned into a pension upon retirement by dividing it by the annuity factor, which depends mainly on cohort life expectancy. The annuity factor is adjusted every year to prevent increased longevity from destabilizing the system.

Second, the notional interest rate depends on the growth of real wages. That is, notional accumulation doesn't grow much if the economy doesn't grow. If real wage growth is less than 1.6 percent per year, then current retirees' benefits are also reduced. If this does not stabilize the system, the automatic adjustment mechanism does. This mechanism adds the notional assets plus the system's buffer fund, and compares this to the present value of pension liabilities. If these assets, both real and notional, are less than the liabilities—this could happen due to falling fertility rates or lower labor force participation rates—then the pension liabilities are reduced. That is to say, the interest rate earned on the notional accounts declines and current benefits also decline. So both future and current beneficiaries immediately bear the burden if the system goes out of long-run balance, thereby restoring balance. But, notice there are no automatic adjustments to the guaranteed minimum, the housing supplements, disability insurance, and other supplements from the government budget. And in fact, those would be expected to increase if economic conditions deteriorate.

So where do the risks of adverse economic and demographic developments go? They are explicitly borne mainly by present and future benefit cuts. In addition, they are implicitly borne by increases in general government spending in amounts not specified ex ante—Kruse and Palmer don't even estimate how the government expenditures might increase under different scenarios.

Looking at where the risks are not borne is also instructive. People with the lowest incomes do not bear the risk because the minimum pension is there to catch them. (Many people receive that minimum pension, and if it continues to be wage indexed, even more may receive it in the future.) The risk will not be borne, either, by an explicit increase in retirement age, although it is assumed that people will retire later when their benefits decrease. An increase in contributions is not an option for restoring financial balance in an NDC plan. In other words, benefits bear most of the brunt of any needed adjustment, which makes sense in a system that has large benefits and a high contribution rate to begin with.

But really, most of the uncertain costs, like the minimum pension and disability benefits, are put into the government budget, and there is no calculation of how those expenditures might change. The authors claim that some of this government spending will increase national saving, which is hard to understand. If spending is financed out of taxes, the higher taxes will offset the higher spending, but if it is financed by deficits, national saving is decreased. In principle, each of these stabilizers could be applied in the United States. We could, for example, shift much of the uncertainty into the government budget, but that would be difficult given our deficits. We could index benefits to longevity (personally, I think we should), but that would be politically difficult. We could, when we find the system is out of balance, automatically reduce benefits. However, we're starting with much smaller benefits and with no minimum benefit, so I doubt that we would want benefits to bear the entire brunt of adjustments.

We could go a step beyond and include contribution rates, benefit rates, and retirement age in an automatic adjustment process. Every year we could compare the expected present discounted value of future expenditures and future revenues. And we could develop a formula for distributing an imbalance (such as we have right now) among benefit cuts, contribution hikes, and so forth. But, the United States would have to specify in much more detail than Sweden what the distributional effects would be, how much would come out of benefits, how much would come out of contributions, and which groups of beneficiaries and taxpayers would be affected most. *This* is really the discussion we should be having. However, given the polarization of political views and the inequality of wages in our country compared with Sweden, it would be much more difficult for us to agree on a formula.

In sum, Sweden has developed a clever system and we should think about some of its elements. But in the end, the differences in our countries' initial conditions will make it difficult to adopt such measures here.

NOTE

1. See, for example, Estelle James, Guillermo Martinez, and Augusto Iglesias, 2006, "The Payout Stage in Chile: Who Annuitizes and Why?" *Journal of Pension Economics and Finance* 5(2): 121–54; Estelle James, Alejandra Cox Edwards, and Rebeca Wong, 2003, "The Gender Impact of Pension Reform," *Journal of Pension Economics and Finance* 2(2):

181–219 (revised version in *Lessons from Pension Reform in the Americas,* forthcoming, edited by Stephen Kay and Tapen Sinha, New York, Oxford University Press); Estelle James and Augusto Iglesias, forthcoming, "Disability Insurance with Pre-Funding and Private Participation: the Chilean Model," draft paper delivered at the International Federation of Pension Funds (FIAP) conference, May 31, 2007, Varna, Bulgaria; Alejandra Cox Edwards and Estelle James, 2007, "Crowd-Out, Adverse Selection, and Information in Annuity Markets: Evidence from a New Retrospective Data Set in Chile," draft ms.; and Alejandra Cox Edwards and Estelle James, 2007, "Did the Chilean Pension Reform Postpone Retirement?" draft ms.

Lawrence H. Thompson

Let me begin by thanking Agneta Kruse and Ed Palmer for giving us a clear and concise description of the new Swedish pension system and explaining the built-in features designed to keep its cost constant and predictable.

One feature adjusts the initial retirement benefit for changes in cohort life expectancy. As expected lifespans increase, monthly benefits are automatically reduced to leave unchanged the present value at retirement of the benefit stream.

A second feature adjusts the calculation of the initial retirement benefit through an algorithm that assures the system's longer-term liabilities don't exceed its projected total assets (including projected future revenues). If projected liabilities appear too large, the accrual rate used in calculating new retirement awards is reduced to bring projected liabilities in line with projected assets.

The third feature alters the size of postretirement adjustments to assure that unanticipated changes in economic growth rates do not produce unanticipated short-range deficits (or surpluses). The extra payroll tax receipts caused by an unanticipated increase in real wage growth are passed on to retirees, whereas the shortfall associated with an unanticipated decrease in the growth rate is covered by curtailing benefit increases.

I also thank Estelle James for her commentary on the desirability of instituting in our own system adjustments that mirror those now incorporated in the Swedish system. I find myself in agreement with many of her points, which those who know both of us will know is a relatively rare situation.

If the United States desired, we could introduce into our own Social Security system automatic adjustments similar in operation and effect to Sweden's. The first two adjustments could be achieved simultaneously by automatically altering the benefit formula each year to bring the 75-year projection of average costs from the Trustees' Report into balance with the report's 75-year income projection. The current benefit formula sets the basic benefit (the Primary Insurance Amount) equal to 90 percent of the first (roughly) $650 of average monthly preretirement earnings, plus 32 percent of the next (roughly) $3,800, plus 15 percent of any remainder.

The easiest way to adjust the formula to guarantee long-range fiscal balance in the face of increasing life expectancies and other economic and demographic uncertainty would be simply to reduce the marginal replacement rate in each of the factors by the constant percentage amount required to bring projected costs in line with projected revenues. Had such a procedure been implemented in 1984, modest adjustments would have been made in the benefit formula in most of the intervening years, and, by now, these adjustments would have had the cumulative effect of cutting initial awards by perhaps 13 percent from today's level.[1] In other words, instead of 90 percent, 32 percent, and 15 percent, the formula for those turning 62 this year would be more like 78 percent, 28 percent, and 13 percent.

If our current long-range projections are reasonably accurate, the pace of reductions under this procedure would accelerate in the future. Under these projections, outlays would have to be reduced by 21 percent (relative to current law) to balance the cash flow in 2035, by 25 percent to balance the 2050 annual flow, and by 30 percent to produce balance in 2080. Under the procedure outlined here, moreover, the reductions instituted in any given year must be large enough not only to cover that year's shortfall, but also to eliminate the shortfall for the following 74 years. Thus, one presumes that this procedure could well end up causing new benefit awards to fall (relative to current law) by almost 30 percent by 2035 and by some 35 percent by 2050.

In our system, the third of the Swedish adjustments would be accomplished by changing the annual benefit increase for those already retired from one based on changes in the consumer price index to one based on movements in average social security earnings. Since our long-range financial projections are based on the assumption that the average wage will grow in the future by 1.1 percentage points faster than the consumer price index, we would subtract 1.1 points from average wage growth to produce the annual adjustment. Had we instituted such a policy in 1995, the annual benefit increases would have been substantially higher in the late 1990s and substantially lower in the early 2000s than was actually the case. The alternative policy would have produced increases averaging 2.9 percent, whereas the actual increases averaged only 2.3 percent. The alternative would also have increased the variability in the annual adjustment. The standard deviation of annual increases would have been 1.7 percentage points under the alternative, compared to 0.6 percent with the actual adjustments. Neither of these differences is very large, however, so we can conclude that this adjustment would not have made much of difference, at least over the last two decades.[2]

Had the two strategies outlined here been implemented in 1983, they could have preserved financial balance in Social Security and assured that the subsequent unanticipated demographic and economic developments did not throw the system out of financial balance. Had they been allowed to operate as designed, they *may* have removed the contentious issue of Social Security reform from the current political agenda and *may* have helped insulate the federal budget from demographic and economic changes. To borrow a phrase much loved by analysts and the World Bank, they would have assured that our Social Security system was "fiscally sustainable"—at least for the time being.

Would introducing these adjustment strategies have been good public policy, however? I think not! First, I fail to the understand the social gain from this particular approach to insulating the federal budget from unexpected economic and demographic changes. Second, I think the mechanism adopted by Sweden to adjust to longer lifespans will eventually produce undesirable results. And, third, I am convinced that our political process would not allow such adjustment to continue for an extended time; in the end, automatic adjustment would fail to achieve its intended result.

My first objection is that under this approach, the federal budget is insulated through the simple expedient of transferring to retirees all uncertainty about both short-range economic developments and longer-range economic and demographic developments. Why we should think that retirees are better able to deal with such uncertainty than is the national government escapes me. There may be some welfare gain from requiring retirees to assume some of this risk, but Sweden's approach makes them assume all of it. In effect, it is a corner solution. It implicitly assumes that there is no social value whatsoever in insulating retirees from uncertainty.

My second objection involves the strategy adopted for dealing with the impact of longer lifespans and falling birthrates, namely reducing the monthly benefit. This approach disadvantages retirees relative to workers and reduces average benefits to levels I consider to be socially undesirable. Although the hypothetical worker who has always earned the average wage is a staple of Social Security program analysis, this hypothetical worker turns out to be substantially better off than the actual average retiree. The Social Security actuaries calculated that the hypothetical average earner retiring in 2004 was entitled to $14,500 a year, which amounted to some 41 percent of the 2004 average wage. In contrast, the actual average retired worker that year received $11,540, or some 32 percent of the average wage. After making the Swedish adjustments, the actual net benefit would fall to about 30 percent of the average wage.

As noted previously, introducing the adjustment strategy now used in Sweden would further reduce average benefits in our system. By 2030, the combination of adjustments could cause the actual average social security net retirement benefit to fall to 20 percent or less of the average wage. (If I interpreted the Kruse–Palmer paper correctly, that would put our *average* benefit at just two-thirds of the Swedish *minimum* pension, relative to the respective average earnings levels.) Personally, I don't believe that reducing monthly benefits to that level is good social policy.

Regardless of my personal views about the desirability of benefits at this level, I would argue that our political system is not likely able to tolerate them. The adjustment mechanism will not, in fact, prove to be fiscally stable because its benefit pattern will not be politically stable. Recently, a similar sequence of events has emerged in two countries that had previously been regarded as having fiscally stable and sustainable public pension programs. I refer to Chile and the United Kingdom. In each, the political system seems to have concluded that their pension programs are now—or in the future, will be—producing inadequate benefits. Each is now considering reforms to improve benefits—with an increase in the respective programs' future cost. Their experience illustrates that, in the end, a pension program cannot be fiscally sustainable if it is does not generate sufficiently generous benefits to make it also socially and politically sustainable.

Some part of the adjustments required to balance Social Security finances will undoubtedly come through increases in payroll tax revenues. The fiscal challenges facing Medicare, however, suggest that a substantial part of the Social Security adjustment will have to come from some source other than payroll tax increases. If monthly benefits have little room for reductions, the only major adjustment left is an increase in the retirement age. If further declines in monthly benefits are to be avoided, however, the increase must include parallel changes in both the early retirement age and the normal retirement age.

Although the normal retirement age in the U.S. system is now rising from 65 to 67, this change is probably more appropriately characterized as a benefit reduction than as a retirement age increase. Benefits will still be available at age 62, albeit with a larger reduction than if the normal retirement age had not been increased, and future retirees are more likely to accept lower benefits than to delay claiming benefits. When the retirement age increase is fully phased in, we should expect that the primary impact will be lower monthly benefits; any delay in the timing of benefit claims probably will be modest. Remember that, for the last 45 years, the U.S. has offered retirees an actuarially fair—better than fair—increase when including the impact of benefit recomputations (i.e., the change in monthly benefits to those willing to postpone collecting until age 65). Only a minority of the retiring population has accepted this offer, however. Based on this experience, I conclude that maintaining monthly benefits at socially acceptable levels is likely to be possible only if the early retirement age is increased in parallel with any increase in the normal retirement age.[3]

In summary, I am not particularly enamored with the way Sweden calculates postretirement benefit adjustments. I don't see the social gain from shifting that particular form of uncertainty from the government to retirees.

I am not opposed to instituting some form of automatic adjustment mechanism to deal with the changes we now foresee in life expectancy and in other future economic and demographic changes that will alter pension program costs. I would not limit the automatic adjustments to essentially changes in monthly benefits, as Sweden has done. Indeed, I would avoid changing monthly benefits and concentrate instead on adjustments in tax rates and retirement ages. I believe that focusing primarily on these other two adjustments is more likely to produce a politically and socially stable arrangement than is focusing on changes in monthly benefit levels, and that political and social stability are prerequisites for financial stability.

Having said that, I must also admit that I do not think it likely that my suggested adjustments would be allowed to go into effect. After all, any automatic adjustment designed to balance future costs and revenues will have to be based on assumptions about future economic and demographic developments as well as the technical aspects of translating those assumptions into cost and revenue estimates. Each of the assumptions and many of the technical decisions can be challenged by politicians that don't like the implications of the calculations. Implementing these sorts of adjustments is far easier when the result of the calculations is a small change in an obscure factor buried in a complicated calculation that is well understood by only a handful of people. Implementing such a change is far more difficult when the result is to change the tax rate for the whole population and the earliest retirement date for an entire birth cohort.

As a final aside, permit me to observe that enhancing Social Security's fiscal stability through the kind of automatic adjustors employed in Sweden could be characterized as a reform to reform the previous reform. During Social Security's first three decades, all program adjustments required specific congressional action. That arrangement maximized fiscal certainty, making it virtually impossible for Social Security ever to run out of money. The arrangement introduced considerable political uncertainty, however, and many believed that the net impact of repeated congressional interventions to adjust benefit levels was higher benefits than would be produced under an indexed system. Automatic indexing of benefits was introduced in 1972, which had the effect of greatly enhancing political certainty at the expense of reducing fiscal certainty. Before 1972, there were no fiscal crises in the program but there were repeated adjustments in the benefit formula. Since 1972, there have been essentially no changes in the benefit formula, but there have been at least two fiscal crises.[4]

Perhaps we just have to resign ourselves to life in an imperfect world.

NOTES

1. Under the assumptions used in the 2005 Trustees' Report (Social Security Administration 2005), average long-range outlays have to fall by 12.2 percent to match average total revenues. Since the benefit adjustments are prospective, the adjustment to the benefit formula would have to be slightly larger to produce the same average reduction over the 75-year projection. If the calculation is made each year, however, the cumulative difference shouldn't be all that large.

2. The impact of this adjustment would be more significant during a period when real earnings fell, as was the case in the mid-1970s, because it would prevent average benefits from rising faster than average earnings.

3. Presumably, continued reductions in the age-62 replacement rate would eventually produce significant voluntary delays in benefit receipt, but I suspect that we would see

a political reaction to perceived inadequate retirement incomes before we see a significant behavioral response among new retirees.

4. Fixing a flaw in the 1972 approach required introducing another calculation method in 1977, but the formula introduced at that time was designed to reproduce the benefit structure adopted in 1972. Legislation adopted in 1983 increased the normal retirement age but did not change the basic benefit formula.

REFERENCE

Social Security Administration. 2005. *2005 Annual Report of the Board of Trustees of the Federal Old-Age and Survivors Insurance and Disability Insurance Trust Funds.* Washington, DC: U.S. Government Printing Office.

3

Japan

Tetsuo Kabe

apan's population decreased in 2005, two years earlier than expected, for the first time since World War II. It will continue to decrease in the coming decades due to a low fertility rate and an aging society. By 2050, the total population will have decreased by 20.7 percent, from 127 million in 2000 to 101 million. People older than 65, who accounted for 17.4 percent of the total population in 2000, will account for 35.7 percent (figure 3.1). By then, the size of and growth in Japan's aged population will have exceeded that of other developed countries (figure 3.2).

This aging population causes huge challenges for Japan's public pension system, public medical insurance system, public long-term care insurance system, and a budget already deep in deficits. Now at the global forefront of dealing with the challenges of an aging society, Japan is trying to be the first to succeed, rather than the first to fail, in such efforts.

This chapter illustrates Japan's public pension system and efforts to reform it, with emphases on (1) mandatory review every five years, obligated by legislation, of the public pensions' financial status, which has often triggered and helped complete reforms, and (2) the automatic adjustment of benefit levels by fixing final pension premium levels and implementing adjustment indexation, which takes into account the decline in number of those paying into the system and the improvement in life expectancy.

Figure 3.1. Japanese Population Trends by Age Group, 1950–2100

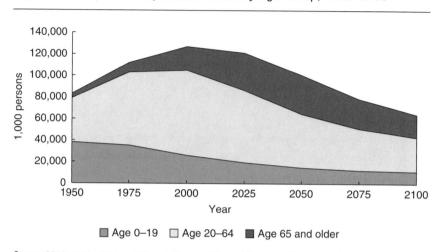

Source: National Institute of Population and Social Security Research (2002).

Figure 3.2. Population Aging in the G5 Countries, 1995–2025 (percent of people older than 65 in the population)

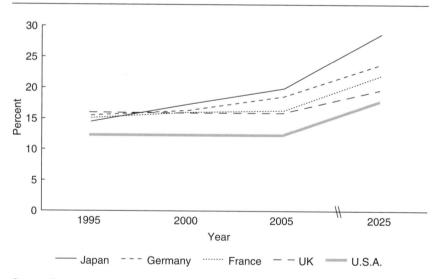

Sources: Figures for Japan are from National Institute of Population and Social Security Research (2002). Figures for other nations are from United Nations projections.

Japan's Social Insurance System

Japan's social insurance system includes the public pension system, the public medical care insurance system, and the public long-term care insurance system, all of which are financed partly by insurance premiums and partly by subsidies from national or local governments.

Public Pension Systems

Everyone older than 20 is required to enroll in the public pension system. It consists of the National Pension System, which includes the Basic Pension and covers everyone, and the Employees' Pension Insurance and Mutual Aid pensions, two earnings-related components for workers. All are defined benefit pensions. Employees' Pension Insurance covers employees of private corporations and Mutual Aid pensions cover public employees and private school employees (table 3.1).

Self-employed persons and farmers are only required to enroll in the National Pension System. They are required to pay fixed pension

Table 3.1. Categories and Premiums for Japan's Public Pension System (standard as of October 2004)

Occupation	Schemes	Premium
Self-employed persons, farmers, students, etc. (20–60 years old)	National Pension	¥13,300 per month
Private-sector employees younger than 65	National Pension and Employees' Pension Insurance	13.934% of total remunerations that combine monthly income and bonuses Evenly borne by employers and employees
Public employees and private school employees	National Pension and Mutual Aid pension	Varies by mutual aid association, ranging from 10.46% to 14.38% of monthly income and bonuses Evenly borne by employers and employees
Spouses supported mainly through an employee's income	National Pension	Paid by the employees' Employees' Pension Insurance or Mutual Aid pension

Source: Pension Bureau (2005).

premiums of ¥13,300 per month, and in return, receive fixed payments of ¥66,208 per month.[1]

Workers are required to enroll in both the National Pension System and an earnings-related pension, either Employees' Pension Insurance or Mutual Aid pensions, depending on their industry. In the case of private-sector employees, workers are required to pay earnings-related pension premiums (13.934 percent of annual wages), which cover both the National Pension System and Employees' Pension Insurance. In return, they receive their first-tier benefit, the Basic Pension, in a fixed amount of ¥66,208 per month; they also receive a second-tier, earnings-related proportional benefit. The model pension payment of ¥233,300 per month is for a household consisting of one worker who earned an average salary for 40 years and a nonworking spouse.

Employees' Pension Insurance is financed through what has been called a modified funded system. The scheme was originally designed in the 1940s as a funded system, but its financing has gradually changed, as benefits were improved and, lately, the society has aged without a sufficient and timely increase in premiums. The pension's financing so heavily relies on premiums collected from the current working generations that it is practically a pay-as-you-go system of intergenerational support, rendering it vulnerable to demographic changes. Today, Employees' Pension Insurance carries a fund equal to about only five years of benefit payments, to improve its intergenerational equity.

Private Pension Systems

More than 166 corporations as of March 2006 provide the Employees' Pension Fund, a private, defined benefit corporate pension and partial substitute for Employees' Pension Insurance. Individuals and enterprises may also opt to enroll in other types of private pension plans, such as the defined benefit corporate pension, the defined contribution corporate pension, the defined benefit personal pension (i.e., the National Pension Fund), or the defined contribution personal pension.

Recent Reforms and the Political, Economic, and Overall Budget Environment[2]

Before 1985

From the inception of Employees' Pension Insurance in 1942 until the 1970s, Japan's public pension system had expanded coverage and improved

Figure 3.3. Real Growth in Japanese Gross Domestic Product, 1956–2004 (percent)

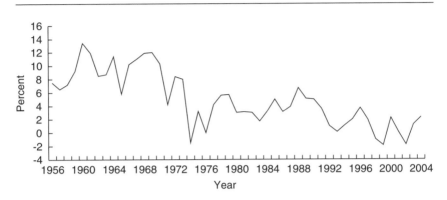

Sources: Lincoln (2005); quarterly estimates of gross domestic product, Cabinet Office, Government of Japan (2004, 2005).

benefits, enabled by high economic growth and an age distribution favorable to a modified funded system or a pay-as-you-go system.

Most notably, the National Pension System was implemented in 1961 to cover self-employed workers and farmers who had not been covered by any public pension (previously, the public pensions had covered employees exclusively). As a result, the Japanese pension system became universal, in that everyone was able to enroll in a public pension. But such an industry-oriented, divided system was vulnerable to demographic movements across industries.

The 1985 reform was introduced as a part of the broader administrative and fiscal reform triggered by the end of high economic growth in the early 1970s, the accumulation of national debt, and the aging of Japanese society (figure 3.3).

The 1985 Reform

Since 1985, the public pension system in Japan has been repeatedly reformed to achieve financial sustainability, in response to an aging society and a much lower rate of economic growth than in the past.[3]

The 1985 reform established a nationally common Basic Pension system by reorganizing the National Pension System. Previously, first-tier, fixed-amount benefits for workers were provided by the Employees' Pension Insurance and Mutual Aid pensions. Now the National Pension

System would provide these benefits not only to self-employed workers and farmers, but to all workers. In this way all public pensions were financially and statutorily integrated in a first-tier, fixed-amount benefit as the Basic Pension. This strengthened the public pensions' financial stability by making them less vulnerable to demographic movements across industries. The reform also adjusted benefit levels by extending the full participating period from 25 years to 40 years.

At the time of the reform, the age of pension eligibility was 65 years for men and women for the Basic Pension, and 60 years for men for Employees' Pension Insurance. The reform raised women's age of eligibility for Employees' Pension Insurance from 55 to 60 years gradually by 2000.

The 1994 Reform

During the late 1980s, Japan's high economic growth, driven by a bubble economy, aided the fiscal consolidation of its national budget, including the budget for public pensions. The population had aged substantially when compared with the past (but not substantially when compared with today's situation). Another major reform to improve the public pension system's fiscal sustainability was not necessary until 1994.

The Japanese government voluntarily conducts demographic projections every five years based on the National Census (also conducted every five years). These projections have revealed a lower-than-expected fertility rate and a longer-than-anticipated life expectancy since 1992. Consequently, actuarial valuations based on the most recent demographic projections have in the past two decades necessitated public pension reforms.

The 1994 reform (like the 2000 reform and 2004 reform) was implemented during the 15 years of economic struggle after the bursting of the bubble economy, when deep deficits resulted from declining tax revenues and increased expenditures as the actual and projected aging of Japanese society progressed (figure 3.4).

Before the 1994 reform, pension premiums were projected to be raised gradually from the current 11.2 percent of annual wages, including bonuses (i.e., 14.5 percent of monthly wages without bonuses), to 26.8 percent of annual wages, including bonuses (i.e., 34.8 percent of monthly wages without bonuses), so that future pension benefits would be maintained as stipulated. The reform cut benefits and increased pension pre-

Figure 3.4. Tax Revenues, Total Expenditures, and Government Bond Issues in the Japanese General Account, 1983–2006 (¥, trillions)

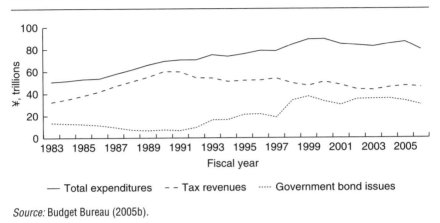

— Total expenditures   – – Tax revenues   ····· Government bond issues

Source: Budget Bureau (2005b).

miums more rapidly, by 1.9 percent of annual wages, including bonuses (i.e., 2.5 percent of monthly wages without bonuses), rather than by 1.7 percent of annual wages, including bonuses (i.e., 2.2 percent of monthly wages without bonuses), every five years, and thus was successful in lowering the projected final pension premium level to 22.9 percent of annual wages, including bonuses (i.e., 29.8 percent of monthly salary without bonuses).

To achieve the required benefit cuts, the 1994 reform gradually raised eligibility age from 60 to 65 years old for the fixed-amount portion of Employees' Pension Insurance, by 2013 for men and by 2018 for women. It also based indexation of benefits on disposable income (wages minus taxes and social insurance premiums), rather than wages. To increase revenue, the reform created special pension premiums (1 percent) levied on bonuses.

The 2000 Reform

The January 1997 demographic projection on aging darkened the outlook on public pensions much more than the prior five-year projection had. If future pension benefits were to be maintained as stipulated, pension premiums would have to have been raised gradually from 13.58 percent of annual wages (17.35 percent of monthly wages) to 26.5 percent of annual wages (34.3 percent of monthly wages). In other words, in the indefinite horizon, ¥530 trillion (or one-fourth of the ¥2,140 trillion projected total liability of the Employees' Pension Insurance) was unfunded in net present value terms (Pension Bureau 1998).

The reform plan eliminated the ¥530 trillion—over 100 percent of gross domestic product (GDP)—in unfunded liabilities by cutting total future benefits by roughly 20 percent and raising pension premiums gradually. Seeking to close the financial gap by equally sharing the pain between retirees and working generations, the reform succeeded in lowering projected future final pension premiums by roughly 20 percent, from 26.5 percent of annual wages (34.3 percent of monthly wages) to 20 percent of annual wages (26.0 percent of monthly wages) (Pension Bureau 1999).

As for benefits, the reform has been gradually raising eligibility age for the earnings-related proportional part of Employees' Pension Insurance, from 60 to 65 years by 2025 for men and by 2030 for women.

The 2000 reform changed indexation of current recipients' pension benefits from being based on disposable income to being based on price. Before the reform, the pension benefits of not only new recipients, but also current recipients, were indexed every five years based on disposable income, in addition to annual indexation based on price. The reform also phased in a 5 percent cut in benefits for the earnings-related part of Employees' Pension Insurance. The phase-in was designed to prevent cuts in nominal benefits. The reform also expanded Employees' Pension Insurance coverage for active workers from 65 to 69 years old and made them subject to collection of pension premiums.

Although discussion for the 2000 reform started in 1996 and was reflected in the 1998 Fiscal Structural Reform Law, that law was suspended in 1999 due to a severe economic downturn largely triggered by the Asian currency crisis and the domestic financial crisis. The bills for the 2000 reform were introduced to the National Diet of Japan (its congress) independent from the suspended discussion on broader fiscal consolidation.

The reform legislation faced political difficulties, partly because it intended to cut benefits and raise the eligibility age again—incurring criticism from opposition parties and labor unions—and partly because increasing pension premiums could have had adverse effects in a deteriorating economy. Despite delayed passage and suspended pension premium increases, the bill was passed by the Diet and became a public law.

Generally speaking, lower economic growth tends to demonstrate, through more-pessimistic projections, the potential vulnerability of the pension system and the need for reform to sustain it. However, a significant economic downturn makes it tougher to implement measures, such as benefit cuts and pension premium increases, that could have negative macroeconomic impacts.

The 2004 Reform

The revised population projection from January 2002 revealed that demographic change was progressing, again more rapidly than anticipated. Based on the new projection, pension premiums would have to be raised to 25.9 percent of annual wages instead of the previously expected 20 percent, if future benefits were to be maintained as stipulated. If future benefits were maintained without increasing pension premiums, Employees' Pension Insurance assets would be exhausted in 2021.

The 2004 reform aimed to balance benefits and contributions over the next 100 years (General Affairs 2005). First, it fixed the final pension premium level from 2017 onward at 18.3 percent of annual wages; until then, pension premiums were to be raised by 0.354 percent every year. Second, to minimize future revisions of benefits and premiums, the 2004 reform incorporated automatic adjustment indexation to help the system adapt to social and economic changes. Third, a plan to raise the national subsidy to the Basic Pension from one-third to one-half of its payments was also adopted, with the subsidy being progressively raised from FY 2004 until no later than FY 2009, following a fundamental reform of the tax system to secure a required stable revenue source. The 2004 reform again improved the public pension's fiscal position by over 100 percent of GDP in net present value terms.

The rapid aging of Japanese society is projected to push up the ratio of social security benefits—public pension, public medical care, public long-term care, and other welfare services—to national income from the current 23.5 percent to 29.0 percent in 2025. If the 2004 public pension reform had not been implemented, the ratio would have reached 31.5 percent in 2025 (figure 3.5).[4]

Figure 3.5. Costs of Japanese Social Security Benefits, Social Security Benefits as a Percentage of National Income, 2000–2025 (¥, trillions)

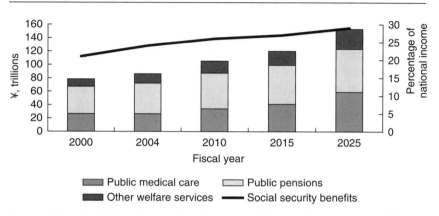

Sources: Watanabe (2006); calculations from the Japanese Ministry of Health, Labour and Welfare (2004).

Note: Long-term medical care is included in the category of other welfare services.

The 2004 reform bills triggered heated debate on the public pension and its future. Most of all, nonregistrations and nonpayments for the National Pension solidified into a major political issue.[5] Whether the National Pension should be financed by pension premiums and general revenues or entirely by a consumption tax, and whether all public pensions should be integrated into one system were also debated. In addition to legislated reforms, measures were taken to improve compliance with laws on paying premiums and the Social Insurance Agency was to be reformed. Although dialogue between the ruling parties and the opposition parties was to continue, the bill was passed by the Diet and became law.[6]

Periodic Mandatory Review of Pensions

In Japan's case, as described above, all recent major pension reforms were triggered by the review of the public pensions' financial status conducted every five years.[7] This legislative requirement also greatly helped the reforms gain political acceptance.

Table 3.2. Demographic Assumptions Used in the 2004 Actuarial Valuation of the Japanese Public Pension System

	2000 (actual)	2050 (projected)
Fertility rate (births per woman in her lifetime)	1.36	1.39
Life expectancy at birth (years)		
Male	77.64	80.85
Female	84.62	89.22
Labor force participation rate (%)[a]		
Men ages 60–64	72.0	85.0
Women ages 30–34	58.8	65.0

Source: Actuarial Affairs Division (2005).

a. Labor force participation rates are projected to change substantially in the age ranges specified for each gender.

Both the Employees' Pension Insurance Law and the National Pension Law require the Japanese government to review the pension programs' current financial status and future financial projections at least every five years and to publish the results of such reviews without any delay. The 2004 reform specifies the projection period as 100 years. Both laws also require each pension program to maintain financial balance in the long term and, in case that financial balance is lost, to immediately take measures to restore it.

Following these provisions, the government reviews financial status and projections based on the updated economic and demographic assumptions (table 3.2, table 3.3). When the government finds that required increases in future pension premiums are unbearable, it proposes options for reform and compiles a reform plan in consultation with the Social Security Council and the ruling parties.[8] In the political process of preparing a reform bill and debating it in the Diet, many conflicting views get aired. Because benefit cuts and premium increases will fall on everyone, such a reform bill is all the more painful. Yet, all parties understand that they have a legal obligation every five years to find a solution, which helps a reform bill toward its final approval by the Diet.

Table 3.3. Economic Assumptions Used in the 2004 Actuarial Valuation of the Japanese Pension System (percent)

	2003	2004	2005	2006	2007	2008	From 2009
	(actual)		(projected)				
Price inflation	−0.3	−0.2	0.5	1.2	1.5	1.9	1.0
Rate of investment return	0.8	0.9	1.6	2.3	2.6	3.0	3.2
Rate of wage growth	0.0	0.6	1.3	2.0	2.3	2.7	2.1
(Real)	(0.3)	(0.8)	(0.8)	(0.8)	(0.8)	(0.8)	(1.1)
Difference between rate of wage growth and rate of investment growth	0.8	0.3	0.3	0.3	0.3	0.3	1.1

Source: Actuarial Affairs Division (2005).

Automatic Adjustment of Benefit Levels

The 2004 reform introduced automatic adjustment of benefit levels by fixing final pension premium levels and implementing adjustment indexation.[9]

Before the 2004 reform, the Employees' Pension Insurance Law showed tables for pension premium increases only for the coming five years, even though projections for pension premium increases were made for the indefinite future. The 2004 law explicitly prescribed that a table be calculated for pension premium increases for the next 100 years. The table shows that pension premiums will be raised by 0.354 percent every year; the final pension premium level from 2017 and onward was fixed at 18.3 percent of annual wages. The law explicitly stipulates these increases to appease younger people's concerns about how high the tax might become.

With the future premium being specifically fixed, benefits are to be automatically adjusted within the revenues. Adjustment indexation serves to implement such automatic adjustment. It modifies the indexation, taking into account the decline in number of those paying into the system and the improvement in older people's life expectancy. For new pension recipients, indexation is based on the per capita growth rate in disposable income minus the adjustment rate. For those already receiving a pension, indexation is based on price minus the adjustment rate. The adjustment rate is around 0.9 percent until 2023, according to the benchmark scenario. The Basic Pension is also subject to adjustment indexation.

Termination of the benefit-level adjustment is determined by projecting socioeconomic trends, taking into account the conditions at each actuarial valuation every five or fewer years, and assessing whether pension finances would be balanced with benefit-level adjustment termination. If socioeconomic conditions improve, then it will be possible to terminate benefit-level adjustment earlier and maintain benefits. Conversely, if the situation deteriorates, adjustment will have to be continued longer than planned, and subsequent benefits will be lower.

Adjustment indexation is carefully designed in two ways not to impair retirees' income security. First, it does not reduce nominal benefits below the level of existing benefits, nor does it function if regular indexation—whether based on disposable income or price—is negative. Second, the replacement ratio of the model pension (the pension for a household consisting of one worker earning an average salary for 40 years and a non-working spouse for 40 years), which is now 59.3 percent, shall not fall below 50 percent. Under adjustment indexation, the nominal pension amount will not be reduced but the replacement ratio, which is the model benefit amount against average net income, will gradually decrease. If the replacement ratio is projected to fall below 50 percent before the next actuarial valuation, benefit-level adjustment termination should be examined (and possibly halted) or different measures adopted based on the findings. The law also stipulates that benefits and premiums as a whole should be reviewed and necessary measures should be taken.

By introducing automatic adjustment of benefit levels, we can now prevent unexpected changes in demographic projections from causing frequent reforms. Japan has learned from having so many consecutive reforms. Such automatic adjustment improves both retirees' and younger generations' confidence in the future of public pensions.

Methods of Financial Projection

The approaches to long-term projection of pension finances fall into two camps: the whole-future-balancing method, which seeks to balance finances over an infinite future period, and the closed-period-balancing method, which balances finances over a finite fixed period.

The 2000 reform adopted the whole-future-balancing method. Although this approach has the merit of taking into consideration all future events, it could bring much uncertainty into the calculations— and it is debatable whether an indefinite future should be considered in the first place. Further, Japan's public pension system has been designed to manage huge assets and to use investment profits to cope with considerable future population aging. Such projection raises the question of whether the public would accept adjustments to their benefits while the government is holding huge assets.

Due to those factors, the closed-period-balancing method was adopted in the 2004 reform. The law stipulates that the fixed period be around 100 years from the time of the valuation. Such a time frame would practically cover all payments to those born at the time of projection. Assets left at the end of this financial balancing period will function merely as a payment reserve. Thus, pension assets in 2100 are projected to be equivalent to only one year of expenditures.

Communication to the Public

To communicate with the public and the press (as well as with policy-makers) on the need for reform, Japan's projection of future pension premiums depicts serious financing problems in a manner the public can imagine in their daily lives. For example, when presenting alternatives for reform, the projection asks citizens, "Are you willing to pay pension premiums twice as high as now, or would you rather accept lower pension benefits?" Such a presentation helps the public realize the problem clearly.

Japan also uses projections of pension liabilities and assets on a net present value basis, which is well understood by economists and scholars but should be explained when communicating with the general public. Educating the public is especially useful when debating alternatives, such as personal accounts. The government also uses cash-flow analysis, but not as often as projection of future pension premiums, since it better communicates the need to minimize intergenerational inequity.

The process of compiling a reform plan involves holding hearings and soliciting public comments, in addition to consulting with the Social Security Council and the ruling parties. With the 2000 reform, five alternatives were presented to the public early in the discussion: (1) maintaining benefits (pension premiums would be raised gradually from 13.58 percent of annual wages to 26.4 percent), (2) cutting benefits by 10 percent (pension premiums would be raised gradually from 13.58 percent to 23 percent), (3) cutting benefits by 20 percent (pension premiums would be raised gradually from 13.58 percent to 20 percent), (4) cutting benefits by 40 percent (pension premiums would not be raised at all), and (5) privatizing Employees' Pension Insurance (Pension Bureau 1998). The alternatives were accompanied by specific options for cutting benefits, including raising eligibility ages, changing indexations, and cutting benefit levels. After repeated open and public discussions, the third alternative was adopted and specific measures to cut benefits were chosen.

By the 2004 reform, the government had begun periodically mailing pension information, including records of premiums, to insured persons. The goal is to promote better understanding by working generations, whose support for the pay-as-you-go public pension is desperately needed, and to make younger generations more aware of the pensions' importance.

Public Pensions in Connection with the Budget

The Employees' Pension Insurance has its own special account separate from the General Account and has its own revenues from pension premiums. However, since one-third of the first-tier fixed amount part (the Basic Pension) is financed by the subsidy from general revenues, it has a large impact on the entire budget.

In FY 2006, expenditures for social security accounted for 25.8 percent—the largest share—of total expenditures from the General Account (figure 3.6). Social security; education, science, and technology; and national debt service are the only three areas where the budget, constructed in a fiscal-consolidation effort, increased in FY 2006.

In addition, the 2004 reform included a plan for the long-debated increase in the national subsidy to the Basic Pension. Such change impacts both the General Account's tax revenues and expenditures and makes public pensions and the General Account more closely related. Under these circumstances, the growing impact of the public pension and other social security programs on the budget has closely connected them with the entire budget.[10]

Figure 3.6. Japanese General Account Budget, Fiscal Year 2006 (¥, billions)

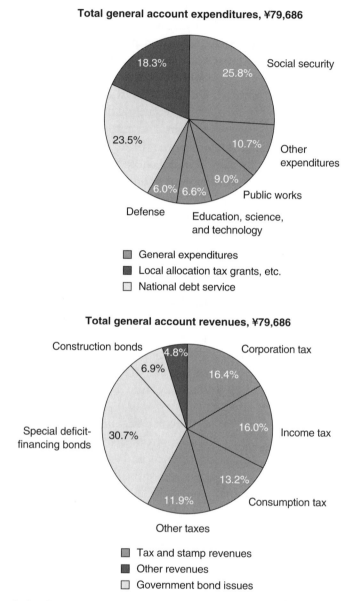

Total general account expenditures, ¥79,686

Social security 25.8%

Other expenditures 10.7%

Public works 9.0%

Education, science, and technology 6.6%

Defense 6.0%

23.5%

18.3%

☐ General expenditures
■ Local allocation tax grants, etc.
☐ National debt service

Total general account revenues, ¥79,686

Construction bonds

4.8%

6.9%

Corporation tax 16.4%

Special deficit-financing bonds 30.7%

Income tax 16.0%

Consumption tax 13.2%

Other taxes 11.9%

☐ Tax and stamp revenues
■ Other revenues
☐ Government bond issues

Source: Budget Bureau (2005a).

NOTES

1. Premiums and payments described in this section are as of October 2004.

2. This discussion mainly focuses on the financial sustainability of Employees' Pension Insurance reforms, although other reforms were made.

3. Recent major reforms that significantly improved the public pensions' fiscal condition were implemented in 1985, 1994, 2000, and 2004.

4. Public pension reform constitutes a significant part of a broader social security reform agenda. Long-Term Care Insurance revised room and board costs and costs borne by care recipients in 2005 and reduced long-term care fees in 2006. Public Medical Care Insurance increased copayments for those older than 70, revised room and board costs for hospitalized patients, and cut medical care fees in 2006.

5. According to a 2002 survey, 5.5 percent of people required to register for public pensions were not registered or were in arrears. Payment rates for the National Pension and the Employees' Pension were 62.8 percent and 97.6 percent, respectively (General Affairs 2005).

6. The 2004 reform left such remaining issues as integration of the Employees' Pension Insurance and Mutual Aid pensions. The bill for integration is scheduled to be submitted to the Diet in 2007.

7. Penner and Steuerle (2004) referred to the five-year mandatory review of the Japanese public pension as an example of the "mandate-a-proposal approach" to controlling entitlements.

8. The Social Security Council is an advisory council of the Ministry of Health, Labour and Welfare that includes scholars, economists, actuaries, and representatives of management, labor unions, and the media.

9. The automatic adjustment of benefit levels introduced by the 2004 reform was categorized by Penner and Steuerle (2004) as an example of the "automatic adjustment approach" to controlling entitlements.

10. For further information on the impact of social security programs on the entire budget, see Kabe (2005).

REFERENCES

Actuarial Affairs Division, Pension Bureau, Ministry of Health, Labour and Welfare. 2005. *Outline of the 2004 Actuarial Valuation on Employees' Pension Insurance and National Pension in Japan.* Tokyo: Ministry of Health, Labour and Welfare.

Budget Bureau, Ministry of Finance. 2005a. *Current Japanese Fiscal Conditions and Issues to Be Considered.* Tokyo: Ministry of Finance.

———. 2005b. *Highlights of the Budget for FY2006.* Tokyo: Ministry of Finance.

General Affairs Division, Pension Bureau, Ministry of Health, Labour and Welfare. 2005. "Brief Overview of the 2004 Pension Plan Revision." Tokyo: Ministry of Health, Labour and Welfare.

Kabe, Tetsuo. 2005. "Japan's Fiscal Challenges and Options for Fiscal Consolidation." Paper presented at the Conference on the Long-Term Budget Challenge: Public Finance and Fiscal Sustainability in the G-7, Washington, DC, June 2–4.

Lincoln, Edward J. 2005. "Japan: Long-Term Budget Challenge." Paper presented at the Conference on the Long-Term Budget Challenge: Public Finance and Fiscal Sustainability in the G-7, Washington, DC, June 2–4.

National Institute of Population and Social Security Research, Government of Japan. 2002. *Population Projections for Japan: 2001–2050.* Tokyo: Government of Japan.

Penner, Rudolph G., and C. Eugene Steuerle. 2004. *Budget Rules.* Research Report. Washington, DC: The Urban Institute. http://www.urban.org/url.cfm?ID=1000668.

Pension Bureau, Ministry of Health and Welfare. 1998. "Choosing Public Pension in the 21st Century." Tokyo: Ministry of Health and Welfare.

———. 1999. "Establishing Public Pension in the 21st Century." Tokyo: Ministry of Health and Welfare.

Pension Bureau, Ministry of Health, Labour and Welfare. 2005. *Textbook for the Study Programme for the Asian Social Insurance Administration.* Tokyo: Ministry of Health, Labour and Welfare.

Watanabe, Hiroshi. 2006. "The Japanese Economy and Fiscal Policy in a Global Economic Environment." Tokyo: Ministry of Finance.

Jagadeesh Gokhale

This chapter provides a well-organized and, given its brevity, surprisingly comprehensive review of the history of reforms to the Japanese public pension insurance program. It first outlines the structure of the Japanese social security system, which includes the medical and long-term care insurance programs, and then focuses on the public pension insurance system.

The Japanese public pension system is composed of three elements—the basic pension that covers everyone over the age of 20 and provides a fixed basic benefit to all, regardless of workforce participation; the employees' pension insurance system, which provides benefits proportional to worker earnings; and a mutual aid insurance program that covers farmers and other self-employed persons.

Japan is undergoing the most pronounced demographic transition in the entire developed world (except, perhaps, in Italy). Japan's overall population began declining in 2005. This decline has been accompanied by a steep increase in the proportion of retirees in the population and by declines in the proportions of workers and children. The decline in the proportion of children points to a sustained transition—one unlikely to end even after another three or four decades.

Japan's public pension insurance system has a history parallel to that of the Social Security system in the United States. The Japanese pension system started in 1942, about two years after the U.S. Social Security program started paying out benefits. The Japanese pension system expanded coverage and increased benefits through the 1970s (as in the United States) and has since faced chronic financial shortfalls, again, similar to the U.S.

The chapter evokes elation and depression at the same time: it describes a society making hard decisions to deal with the demographic and fiscal challenges that it faces. Since 1985, the Japanese government has undertaken four public pension reforms. This stands in sharp contrast to the frustrating deadlock on the issue of Social Security reform in the United States. Why the difference? The quick answer is that the legal framework surrounding the Japanese public pension system "obligates" the government to undertake a periodic review of the system's finances and immediately fix the serious long-term imbalances that actuarial analysis reveals. But that raises the further question of why such a legal framework exists in Japan but not in the United States. One could only speculate inconclusively about the answer to that question.

In 1985, projected population aging and slower expected economic growth triggered public pension reform in Japan. This reform streamlined the basic pension across programs for different participants and reduced retirement benefits by increasing the ages of eligibility for various types of benefits.

Projected demographic changes and program finances did not worsen again until 1992. Since then, however, actuarial analysis has repeatedly revealed worsening pension finances due to demographic factors—lower fertility and rising longevity—and this despite several attempts to restore sustainability to the public pension program.

As a result, reforms were periodically mandated to occur in 1994, 2000, and 2004. However, each time, changes to premiums and benefits were found to be inadequate during the next legally mandated actuarial evaluation.

The chapter does not describe or speculate about why this may have occurred. Rapid and ongoing changes could have rendered the task of making precise demographic and financial projections difficult. Alternatively, the reforms enacted may not have been fully implemented because of exceptional economic conditions.

It is instructive that Japanese official analysts calculated financial shortfalls in perpetuity, rather than through a limited time horizon of 75 or 100 years. It is also noteworthy that in Japan, public pension reforms targeted elimination of the entire infinite-horizon unfunded liability. The failure to achieve sustainability despite using comprehensive measures of funding shortfalls shows not that such measures are inappropriate, but just that they do not necessarily lead to policy changes sufficient to achieve sustainability. Had Japanese policymakers used short-horizon measures (such as the 75-year measures used in the United States), reforms may have been even less ambitious and larger financial gaps could have remained, making future adjustments more costly.

Repeatedly reforming the system only to find that the reforms fell short taught the Japanese another lesson—that they needed to undertake "smart" reforms. They have since introduced flexible policy rules designed to adjust pension budget flows automatically in response to demographic changes. These types of measures have three advantages:

(1) The measures prevent delays in implementing reforms that would make achieving a program's financial balance more expensive.
(2) The communication of a clear fiscal adjustment rule allows households to appreciate the true degree of uncertainty that they face and that is embodied even in public pension systems. (Participants in the U.S. Social Security program lack such information because that system contains no automatic adjustments to restore Social Security to long-term sustainability if it faces a growing financial imbalance.)
(3) The measures are potentially more consistent with tax smoothing, because quicker adjustments are likely to allocate adjustment costs more evenly across current and future generations.

Despite adopting automatic adjustment factors, however, the 2004 Japanese pension reform also built in constraints on how far those adjustments could be taken. Limits on automatic benefit cuts and premium increases mean that future adjustments may not deliver long-term sustainability to the Japanese public pension system.

In addition, the Japanese have now abandoned pension calculations over the infinite horizon—opting for 100-year projections. This move may have been made because projections show little difference between the imbalances calculated under the two alternatives. Based on U.S. experience, however, this could be a mistake. The United States abandoned infinite-horizon calculations in favor of 75-year projections for the same reason. However, changes to benefit rules, specifically the indexation of retirement benefits to inflation, mean that the 75-year imbalances severely understate the magnitude of Social Security's total financial shortfalls under current laws. In turn, relying on short-term estimates of financial shortfalls in U.S. entitlement programs holds the potential to severely bias reform choices in the United States (see Gokhale and Smetters 2006).

Should the Japanese also adopt a privately funded system for younger individuals? Given the problems associated with maintaining and managing a large public fund for paying future pension benefits, and given that Japanese saving rates have declined from about 10 percent during the 1990s to about 6 percent in the 2000s, perhaps adopting a defined contribution–type system would be appropriate—especially since additional adjustments to the defined benefit system appear inevitable. A mandatory personal accounts system may be a good option for increasing Japanese households' retirement savings, given their apparent unwillingness to increase defined benefit pension premiums beyond 18.3 percent.

The chapter clarifies that the Japanese pension system has built-in features that could benefit other countries facing similar demographically driven fiscal pressures. These include the legal institutions surrounding Japan's public pension programs and a budget process whereby long-term entitlement imbalances automatically trigger policy reforms. Better still would be to adopt automatic adjustment mechanisms that respond to changing demographics to maintain the program's long-term financial balance.

I conclude by drawing attention to another notable feature of Japan's public policy: the emphasis placed on minimizing potentially crippling tax burdens on younger and future generations. Current generations in Japan, including retirees, appear more willing than their counterparts in other countries to make sacrifices despite the greater hardships involved in their daily lives. Perhaps this is because of the greater social cohesion that is the hallmark of Japanese society.

REFERENCE

Gokhale, Jagadeesh, and Kent Smetters. 2006. "Measuring Social Security's Financial Outlook within an Aging Society." *Daedalus* (Winter): 91–104.

Richard Jackson

Japan's new demographic stabilizer, introduced during the 2004 pension reform, represents an essential step toward restoring fiscal sustainability and generational equity to its pension system. Along with similar reforms in Germany and Sweden, it provides a useful model for policymakers in the United States.

Figure C3.1 is based on some particularly revealing numbers included in Tetsuo Kabe's chapter. It shows the projected ultimate contribution rate for the Employees' Pension Insurance system immediately before and after the 1994, 2000, and 2004 reforms. The rate is like one of the punching-bag dolls that children play with—kick it down and it bounces back up. The 1994 reform lowered the projected ultimate contribution rate from 26.8 to 22.9 percent of payroll. But by the eve of the 2000 reform, the ultimate contribution rate had risen back to 26.5 percent. The 2000 reform lowered the projected ultimate contribution rate to 20.0 percent of payroll. But by the eve of the 2004 reform, it had risen back to 25.9 percent. In each case, as Kabe explains, the upward revisions were largely the result of new and less-favorable demographic projections.

The continuing need for reform eventually strained even Japan's legendary capacity for consensus building—and led the government to enact an automatic "demographic stabilizer" as part of the latest 2004 reform. The stabilizer, which in effect indexes the pension system to changes in the ratio of contributing workers to retired beneficiaries, has three great

Figure C3.1. Projected Ultimate Contribution Rates for the Employees' Pension Insurance System, before and after the 1994, 2000, and 2004 Reforms

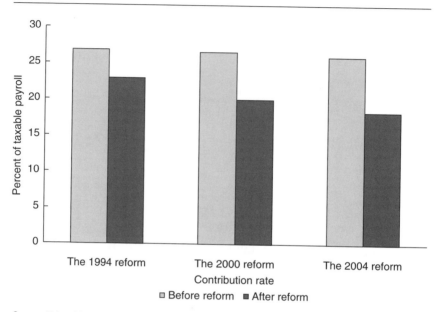

Source: Kabe, this volume.

virtues. It changes the default outcome from cost growth to cost constraint. It generates immediate savings. And, because the benefit reductions it triggers apply to both new and current benefits, it shares the sacrifice among generations.

Pay-as-you-go pension systems in most developed countries are set on a rising autopilot. Since benefits (or at least initial benefit awards) are generally indexed to wages, a falling ratio of workers to retirees automatically translates into a rising cost rate. The Japanese stabilizer creates a new kind of autopilot, one that automatically adjusts benefits so that total costs remain constant as a share of payroll and gross domestic product. Without such a stabilizer, pay-as-you-go pension systems in aging societies precommit a growing share of the economic resources of future generations. With a stabilizer, future generations can decide how best to allocate resources to meet new priorities—an argument that Rudy Penner and Gene Steuerle (2005) have made eloquently in a recent essay.

That said, the 2004 reform falls short of a complete and lasting solution. One problem is that the Japanese pension system is already running a large annual cash deficit. Although the stabilizer is designed to keep the system's cost rate from rising, it does not eliminate this deficit. Moreover, as actually enacted, the stabilizer is only a temporary measure, scheduled to remain in effect until 2025, after which the full prereform benefit formula once again applies.

As figure C3.2 shows, contributions to the Employees' Pension Insurance system currently cover only about two-thirds of annual expenditures. The gap between contributions and expenditures is projected to narrow over the next two decades, as the stabilizer puts the brakes on cost growth and as a series of scheduled increases to the contribution rate kicks in. The gap, however, never closes—and in fact, it begins to widen again rapidly after 2025, when the stabilizer sunsets.

To be sure, the architects of the 2004 reform claim to have balanced the pension system over the next 100 years—or for all intents and purposes,

Figure C3.2. Employees' Pension Insurance Expenditures and Contributions as a Percent of Taxable Payroll, 2005–2100

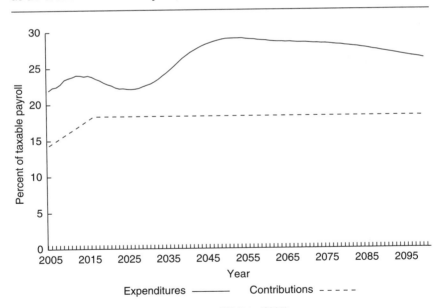

Source: Japanese Ministry of Health, Labour and Welfare (2005).

indefinitely. As can be seen in figure C3.3, however, this balance depends on massive general revenue subsides plus a reserve fund, which from a fiscal and economic perspective amounts to the same thing. Table C3.1 makes the same point another way. It shows the ratio of reserve fund assets to annual expenditures before and after the 2004 reform. Before the reform, the reserve fund was projected to be exhausted in 2021. After the reform, it is projected to be solvent in 2100.

So why is this a problem and not a solution? In brief, the Japanese reserve fund, like the U.S. Social Security trust fund, is little more than a memo account. Historically, the government has failed to translate contributions to the reserve fund into genuine savings—and, despite recent reforms that attempt to build a firewall between the fund and the rest of the budget, there is no guarantee it will do so in the future. Indeed, it stretches credulity to think that the Japanese government (or indeed any government) can refrain from spending, borrowing against, or otherwise nullifying trust-fund savings during a build-up and draw-down scheduled to last for nearly a century.

Figure C3.3. Total Annual Revenue of the Employees' Pension Insurance System, by Source, 2005–2075

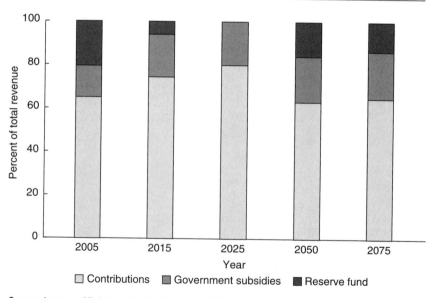

Source: Japanese Ministry of Health, Labour and Welfare (2005).

Table C3.1. Employees' Pension Insurance Reserve Fund Ratio before and after the 2004 Japanese Public Pension Reform, 2005–2100

	Before	After
2005	5.3	5.2
2010	3.8	4.2
2015	2.2	3.9
2020	0.6[a]	4.2
2025	0.0	4.7
2050	0.0	4.5
2075	0.0	2.8
2100	0.0	1.0

Sources: Japanese Ministry of Health, Labour and Welfare (2005).

a. The reserve fund was projected to be exhausted in 2021.

I would like to conclude by broadening the discussion and saying a few words about Japan's aging challenge. We think that we have a big problem in the United States, where, according to the UN's constant fertility scenario, the elder share of the population is due to rise from 12 percent today to 20 percent in 2050. But in Japan, according to the same scenario, the elder share of the population will rise from 20 percent today to 39 percent in 2050. Moreover, the Japanese population is not only due to age dramatically, but to enter a steep decline. By 2050 under the same scenario, there will be 33 percent fewer working-age adults than there are today. The decline among younger entry-level workers will be even greater (United Nations 2005).

Confronting a demographic transformation of this magnitude will require far-reaching changes in Japan's society and economy. Japan's notoriously rigid educational system will have to be overhauled to ensure it remains internationally competitive. Retirement ages will have to go up, immigration will have to rise, and the recent and worrisome decline in Japan's traditional ethic of filial piety will have to be reversed. Perhaps most important, new public policies and private expectations will be required to help women balance jobs and babies. There is now a whole generation of young women in Japan who see little percentage in getting married and having children. If the fertility rate remains at 1.3, there really is no long-term solution.

The place to start, though, is for Japan to regain control over its fiscal future. And here, with the 2004 reform's demographic stabilizer, it has made an impressive start.

REFERENCES

Ministry of Health, Labour and Welfare. 2005. *The 2004 Actuarial Review of the Employees' Pension Insurance and the National Pension.* Tokyo: Ministry of Health, Labour and Welfare.

Penner, Rudolph G., and C. Eugene Steuerle. 2005. "A Radical Proposal for Escaping the Budget Vise." Washington, DC: The Urban Institute. National Budget Issues Brief 3. http://www.urban.org/url.cfm?ID=311192.

United Nations. 2005. *World Population Prospects: The 2004 Revision.* New York: UN Department of Economic and Social Affairs, Population Division.

4

Germany

Michael Mersmann

The multilayered old-age pension system in Germany has evolved over time: a number of reforms since 1990 have improved its fairness and reduced its burden on the budget. As the generosity of the state pension's first pillar has been reduced, other types of pensions have been expanded. The 2001 pension reform substantially expanded additional old-age pensions and introduced the state-supported Riester pension system based on private investments. The 2003–2004 reforms guaranteed that statutory old-age pension funding would be contributed from both workers and federal subsidies and that pension amounts would adjust to wages and economic conditions. These latter reforms responded to less-favorable economic trends and greater increases in life expectancy than were anticipated when the 2001 reforms were adopted.

The 2004 measures reflect proposals put forward by the federal Commission for Sustainable Funding of the Social Security Systems, which included members from academia and socially relevant groups such as labor unions. The German pension system's goal is to assure older citizens a reasonable replacement rate while limiting the need for future tax increases.

Statutory Pension Insurance: The System's First Pillar

The pension system's first pillar, statutory pension insurance, provides the major share of benefits to those who have been insured for many years and gives them a standard of living when retired that relates to their income when working. This general pay-as-you-go, earnings-related first pillar covers around 80 percent of Germany's employed population— 33 million people. With few exceptions, all employees pay compulsory contributions. Even trainees, disabled people employed at sheltered workshops, people on military or civilian service, and those doing a year of voluntary community or environmental service are included.

Recent reforms have reduced the growth of long-term benefits to avoid overburdening future generations. Contribution rates and pensions are set by law until 2030 at a level that ensures the system can be sustained. The reform requires that pretax pension levels not go below 46 percent of average earnings until 2020, or below 43 percent until 2030. Pension levels are calculated for the so-called standard pensioner who has earned the average income for 45 years, paid appropriate contributions, and retired at 65.

The contribution rate is to be held to 20 percent until 2020, and is not to exceed 22 percent up to 2030. Contributions for the child care period (three years after each child's birth) are paid by the government. Workers contributing to the pension system receive annual "earnings points" depending on the amount of their earnings. Someone who earns exactly the average would receive one earnings point for that year's contribution. The value of one earnings point in 2005 was €26.13 (€22.97 in eastern Germany). This value is indexed annually to the growth of gross earnings, but some factors in the adjustment formula may curb the indexation. Pensions are then adjusted to the change in the earnings point value, whether the pensioner is newly retired or not.

After 2008, the German government must report every four years on how to meet the targets for replacement and contribution rates. Changes in eligibility ages may be required. The system is also buttressed by an automatic adjustment mechanism that reduces indexing if the ratio of taxpayers to beneficiaries deteriorates.

By limiting payroll tax increases, the pension reforms greatly helped stabilize wage costs and thus encouraged employment growth. Without reform, the contribution rate would have been one point higher in 2004 than the actual postreform contribution rate, and would have jumped another 0.6 points in 2005. By 2030, the contribution rate will be 2.3 percentage points lower as a result of the reforms.

Certain legal and personal conditions must be satisfied to claim a pension. The regular age to qualify for an old-age pension is 65. The minimum age to receive a pension because of unemployment or reduced work hours will increase from 60 to 63 years from 2006 to 2008, for those born after 1945. Those born after 1951 may no longer draw an early pension because of unemployment or reduced work hours. Future statutory old-age pension insurance only offers the possibility of coverage before age 65 to those with disabilities and those with 35 years of contributions. But those who take an early retirement are penalized with a 0.3 percent monthly reduction. People who postpone retirement past age 65 receive a 0.5 percent monthly bonus increase.

A five-year minimum of contribution periods and substitute contribution periods such as the child care period, with some exceptions, is needed to qualify for a standard old-age pension, a reduced–earning capacity pension, or a surviving dependents' pension. A 15-year minimum of contribution periods and substitute contribution periods is needed to qualify for old-age pension if unemployed or after partial retirement; or for women age 60 and older. The 35-year qualifying period for a long-service pension or severe disability pension can also be made up with such exempt periods as education and training, illness, or unemployment. Child-raising and care periods also qualify workers for receiving the pension.

For those struck by illness and unable to work, the reduced–earning capacity pension can substitute for lost earnings. Working three to six hours a day under normal conditions is considered partial reduced-earning capacity, qualifying the worker for half the rate of the full pension. The full pension, generally paid on a fixed-term basis, is for those who cannot work three hours a day. German pension law expressly puts rehabilitation before a pension, when possible.

Widows and widowers are entitled to a statutory surviving dependents' pension if the deceased spouse qualified for the old-age pension and the survivor remains unmarried. The size of the pension granted depends on the survivor's age and whether he or she has children under 18. Legislation enacted in 2002 set the minimum pension at 25 percent of the deceased spouse's full pension and the maximum at 55 percent. Orphans' pensions are paid up to age 18, or up to age 27 for those in school.

Couples have the option to split their pensions. Married couples who have satisfied the pension credit requirements for 25 years may jointly declare that pension entitlements accrued during their marriage be summed then split evenly between them. Once the decision on pension splitting comes into effect, any entitlement to the surviving dependent's pension ceases.

Occupational Retirement Provision: The System's Second Pillar

The voluntary occupational retirement provision enables workers to save additional funds for retirement. The 2001 pension reform gave employees the right to convert a portion of their incomes into pensions. Contributions can be deducted from taxable income, while withdrawals are taxable. The initial tax deduction decreases the immediate burden on employee income, allowing more funds for old-age savings. Even low-income workers can take advantage of these pensions.

Employers decide how to implement the savings plans. Collective agreements in many sectors of the economy provide for an obligatory occupational retirement plan and may provide financial incentives for employees to save.

The second pillar's attractiveness largely depends on the possibility of taking it with you—on the portability of the capital when changing to other employers. The vesting period for employer-funded entitlements had dropped from ten years to five years as the result of earlier reforms, and the employment age for vesting had dropped from 35 to 30. The 2001 reform made vesting immediate. Portability was improved further in 2005. Now these entitlements can be converted into cash when leaving an old employer and transferred into a new employer's pension system.

After decades of stagnation in private saving for pensions, these reforms and new awareness have encouraged much more of the population to make contributions. Currently, about 10.3 million workers in the private sector and 5.4 million public employees contribute to an occupational pension plan. Roughly 60 percent of workers are now covered. Private-sector coverage rose from 38 percent to 46 percent in the four-year period ending 2004.

Additional Capital-Covered Old-Age Pension Provision: The System's Third Pillar

The 2001 pension reform created a new state-subsidized old-age pension provision known as the Riester pension. Contributions are deductible up to a limit, while withdrawals are taxable. There is also some pension saving out of after-tax income when deductions exceed the limit.

Since the 2001 Riester reform, roughly 11 million new private old-age pension insurance contracts were made with the insurance industry. All beneficiaries can receive a subsidy independent of their earnings, plus an additional special-expenses deduction can be claimed as a tax advantage.

Beneficiaries include everyone ultimately affected by the reduction in state pensions, including employees, recipients of supplementary wage benefits, nonearning parents caring for children, self-employed persons, farmers, and civil servants. Workers pay their own contributions toward a suitable subsidized contract. The state subsidy is credited to their contract when requested by the provider. The pension subsidy consists of a basic subsidy and a child subsidy.

The Riester pension is structured as follows. By 2008, 4 percent of the previous year's income is to be saved annually. This amount is made up of the beneficiary's own savings and a basic subsidy of €154. Where appropriate, a subsidy of €185 per child is added. The personal contributions plus the subsidies can be deducted from tax to a maximum of €2,100 per year. Depending on the recipient's income and number of children, the subsidy is at least 24 percent and can rise to more than 90 percent of the amount saved. So far, the participation rate in the Riester plans has been somewhat disappointing. Perhaps that is because the subsidies are initially quite small, as they phase up to 4 percent of earnings in 2008.

Private old-age pension insurance, and fund and bank saving schemes are eligible for subsidies. Fund and bank saving schemes must be linked to payment plans and a residual pension at higher ages. Further, an occupational old-age provision can be promoted in the shape of direct insurance (*Pensionskassen*) and pension funds.

Maya MacGuineas

As in all counties that have reformed their pension systems to address demographic challenges, the reforms in Germany have yielded mixed results. The United States can learn many lessons by looking at what has worked and what has not as countries around the world have tried to address their solvency challenges and attempted to prefund their pension systems.

When considering solvency first, the European countries are different than the United States in that they start with higher contribution rates. This is certainly the case in Germany. To some, this argues that the U.S. can address the fiscal imbalances in retirement programs in large part on the revenue side. Germany has also moved forward with many sensible measures: it has improved solvency by increasing penalties for early retirement and by changing the average number of years needed to qualify for full retirement. Now it is presumably raising the retirement age.

In addition, German law now requires the government to assess its system every four years and if imbalances are detected, to make proposals for restoring sustainability. The U.S. could certainly benefit from the addition of this type of an oversight mechanism. The U.S. budget is currently divided into discretionary spending and mandatory spending. The mandatory portion of the budget receives a lot less scrutiny than the discretionary portion. The government has no automatic way to examine our programs and to decide whether they are working or whether they are imbalanced.

The United States has seen tense discussions about whether the whole notion of entitlement makes sense, or in other words, whether any programs should be on automatic pilot. A moderate change in that notion, while recognizing the need for our social security system to fulfill its long-term promises, would be to build a German-type reform into our system: a requirement for regular oversight, forcing government to reform the system whenever it became unbalanced. The prescription drug bill built a similar mechanism into Medicare, but Social Security has nothing comparable. Thus, both triggers and defaults could play a very positive role in improving the U.S. Social Security system.

Going further, I think that building in automatic stabilizers—the wave of the future in entitlement reform—is crucial. Benefits and tax rates can, for example, be indexed to things like dependency ratios or expected life. Such mechanisms can keep programs solvent even as demographic or economic factors change unexpectedly.

Automatic stabilizers do bring with them new types of risk, since future taxpayers and recipients are subject to change. This is, however, no different than the situation today, and there is no way to rid any government program of risk. Pension and health care programs are often parts of social contracts that try to spread risk in a useful and practical way. Sometimes, though, programs wrongly perpetuate the notion that we can get rid of risk for participants entirely. We cannot, nor should we, guarantee that programs will remain the same in the future as they are today. Current Congresses cannot bind the hands of future Congresses. We should not even try to make inviolable promises for the long term, particularly when we don't know what factors will be at play in the future. Automatic stabilizers may help programs come closer to meeting their promises by preventing a complete financial collapse that would require radical reforms. But again, there is no way to get rid of risk entirely.

Germany recently created a heavily subsidized prefunded portion of the pension system, called the Riester system. Its take-up rate has been quite low, about one-seventh of what had been anticipated. If the U.S. moves forward with prefunding, either as a part of Social Security or with separate pension plans, we can learn many lessons from the German experience. First, the regulations on these pensions were probably too complex and alienated potential participants. One lesson to be learned is that simplicity is key.

One policy that we might consider is the widespread use of default enrollment. That is to say, a person would be signed up automatically rather than having to take the initiative to enroll him- or herself. The person could then withdraw, if he or she liked. Also, the choice of investments should be fairly limited, as in the American civil service's Thrift Savings Plan. There is always a tradeoff between simplifying investment vehicles and tailoring them to different situations, but simplification has great merit, especially when a new plan is in its early stages. When the savings are eventually converted into a pension, different annuity products could be considered for different family situations or different life expectancies. But when starting a new kind of prefunded program, simplicity will make it much more accessible and less alienating.

While I would argue for simplicity when it comes to the defined contribution portions of pension systems, the reforms to defined benefit programs in many countries have been complicated. Although I am a big believer in transparency in budgeting, it can be easier, politically, not to advertise how hard reform is. I head the Committee for a Responsible Federal Budget, and it often argues that the nation must face up to tough choices. But politicians don't like to talk about tough choices. So when changing a program to improve its solvency, it can be useful to discuss bend points or longevity indexing—things most citizens don't understand. This may be easier than talking about things they do understand, like raising taxes or raising retirement ages. Transparency is clearly good budgeting practice but not generally politically pragmatic.

Another reason that the take-up rate was low for the German Riester plan may have been related to concerns that arose about the riskiness of financial markets after the U.S. stock market bubble burst. Most U.S. proposals for prefunded defined contribution plans do recognize this problem, but there is tension between wanting investors to gain higher returns if they take risks, and preventing those who are more naïve about investing from undertaking far more risk than they realize. Investment programs that have some government backing and are widespread or universal or mandatory should be relatively safe. That can be accomplished by creating highly diversified default investments.

The low take-up rate for Germany's voluntary Riester system suggests that some saving programs should be mandatory. There is strong political resistance to this notion in the United States, but a mandatory program ensures that the people who need most to save sufficiently for retirement are doing so. It also allows us to skip the tricky question of how to design benefit offsets for people who give up all or some portion of benefits to enter an individual defined contribution plan.

Finally, in Germany, despite tax and other subsidies for voluntary saving, people are not saving enough as the public pension system is being cut back. On the one hand, government would like to cut pensions to the bare minimum to address the budget pressures related to demographic changes. But people may still be under the illusion that the public pension system is enough, despite government exhortations that they should save more in a private plan. The true dilemma that I cannot resolve is this: how to maintain a government role in saving while also helping people truly understand that they should be saving more on their own?

The biggest challenge facing Western democracies is how to get politicians to worry as much about the long term as about the short term. Budget process solutions may be useful here. We have already discussed a possible role for automatic stabilizers that preserve solvency over the long run. Alternatively, we might consider a pay-as-you-go rule that requires benefit promises not exceed current tax levels. The world seems ready for new kinds of budget rules that consider the interests of future generations and do not saddle them with financing promises made in the distant past.

Neil Howe

There are some important parallels between the German and the American social security systems. Germany in the early 1950s made an irrevocable decision to go to a totally pay-as-you-go system, as did the U.S., also in the early 1950s. Germany in 1972 enacted a much more generous pension formula and made very early retirement available to most classes of workers. This was also the year in which the U.S. had our final large increase in Social Security benefits—a 20 percent increase, automatic cost-of-living indexing, and all the rest—just before the 1973 OPEC oil embargo shook both countries' economies.

And we both had problems designing reforms. In the U.S., we blundered into something called "double indexing" that caused newly awarded benefits to climb much faster than either wages or prices and made total benefit outlays rise uncontrollably. The problem was solved six years later in 1978 with President Jimmy Carter's Social Security reform. Germany also had some instability because it indexed both its initial benefits and its current benefits to gross wages, which actually included the taxes workers were paying to keep the system going. This arrangement had negative feedback effects because, as taxes rose, the ratio between benefit levels and after-tax wages rose as well. The problem was solved by Chancellor Helmut Kohl's reform in 1992, 20 years later.

There are as well some major differences between the two systems. Most obviously, the German system is much, much larger in that it provides a

70 percent replacement rate (compared with the U.S. rate of 35 to 40 percent). It is, as a share of gross domestic product, two-and-a-half times larger than the U.S. Social Security old-age insurance pension system—the largest among OECD countries, except for Italy's. At the same time, Germany has an extremely low fertility rate, one of the lowest in Europe. It has had a history of very early retirement and a low reliance on funded private pensions. Private-funded assets (that is, pension assets) are only about 10 percent of gross domestic product in Germany, one of the lowest levels of funding for private pensions in Europe.

The system's extreme generosity has necessitated a number of reforms. Those undertaken in 2001 restricted early retirement and made complex adjustments to bring down the long-term replacement rate. And then most recently, the Rürup Commission also recommended a number of reforms. One of the most important was an automatic adjustment called the sustainability factor. This approach provides a unique contribution to our thinking about long-term social security reform.

Just as BMW advertises the "perfectly designed automotive machine," the sustainability factor can be called a perfectly designed pension reform.[1] This new automatic adjustment reduces the benefit both for new pensioners and for current beneficiaries when the ratio of the number of beneficiaries to contributing workers plus the unemployed goes up. Without this adjustment and other reforms affecting the replacement rate, the average pension and the wages of the average worker would correspond exactly at all times, because they would all go up in tandem. For example, if someone started out with a pension equal to 70 percent of the average wage, that ratio would be maintained, even if the person had been retired for 15 years. (This is what makes a wage-wage indexing system like Germany's so inflexible and expensive.) Now, with the sustainability factor, that ratio may erode to something like 60 percent or 55 percent.

The only problem is that the automatic adjustment has only a 25 percent weight (i.e., a weight of 0.25). That is why the sustainability factor will not automatically bring total benefits to a constant share of payroll in future decades. If the formula had a weight of 1.0, it would be the perfect adjustment, thus keeping costs a constant share of wages for the long run.[2]

From an American point of view, Germany's pension system (like many German creations) may seem overengineered; many complicated adjustments in addition to the sustainability factor are aimed at controlling costs. For instance, Germany is increasing the normal retirement age from 65 to 67 without any increase in the minimum retirement age. That is equivalent to a reduction in the replacement rate at any given age. They could have relied entirely on the automatic sustainability factor, and if they were willing to let costs rise a bit relative to wages, they could have given it a weight of 0.5 or 0.7 and then raised it to 1.0 when necessary.

In addition, the Riester reform tried to raise Germany's low participation rate in funded private pensions. Nevertheless, the participation rate remains very low. I totally agree with Maya MacGuineas's commentary: participation should simply be made mandatory. The whole idea is to construct a floor of protection through government intervention. If private pensions are to be part of this floor, they ought to be mandatory.

The final question is whether the German reforms will endure politically. It's easy to enact complex parametric reforms with automatic economic and demographic feedback. The difficult question is, will citizens continue to ratify reductions in benefit growth once they actually find out what's going on? MacGuineas made the point that sometimes it is easier to enact reforms that most people do not understand. Consider the U.S. raising the retirement age in 1982, which (because it was implemented with a long delay and through complex formulas) people had a hard time figuring out. Interestingly, opinion polls have consistently showed that trimming benefits gets a less-negative reaction than raising the "normal" retirement age, even though functionally they're identical. Nobody wants to be told that they can't retire as early as they wanted to. That's always bad politics. But trimming benefits, which saves the system the same amount, is more palatable politically.

One thing that impressed me about the German reform is how much of the crunch hits quickly. The decline in the replacement rate provided by the public pension occurs long before the Riester pensions could possibly replace that income, because of the long buildup time private pensions require.

So an interesting dilemma involves the cohorts born between 1950 and 1970—Germany's Green Party generation, those most shaped by the late 1960s. These cohorts are going to be retiring over the next 20 years. They will be the ones hardest hit by the reforms. Assuming everyone participates in the Riester reform, later-born people will do somewhat better, because their private pensions will have had time to grow.

Philipp Missfelder of the German Christian Democratic Union, leader of its Youth League, recently complained that the German pension system amounts to young people having to pay for the health costs and pensions of old people.[3] But it turns out that under this reform, young people won't be the ones who suffer that much. If the reforms go according to plan, it will be their older brothers and sisters, or maybe their parents, who bear the brunt.

NOTES

1. To understand the role of the sustainability factor, remember that Germany has a generously indexed pay-as-you-go pension system. New pensions are indexed to the current wage, then every year afterward the benefits are indexed to wages. So Germany can be said to have a wage-wage system. Not many exist. The American, Japanese, and Canadian systems are wage-price. That is to say, the initial benefit is determined by a wage index, but after it is granted, it is henceforth indexed to prices. The UK's system can be called a price-price system in that both initial and existing benefits are indexed to prices. (No country uses price-wage indexing. That would be odd.)

2. The automatic adjustments adopted by Italy and Sweden affect the rate at which benefits accrue over the long run, but it is not clear how fast costs respond to the demographic and economic surprises that drive pension systems out of adjustment.

3. See, for example, Mark Landler, "German Youth Leader Urges: Let Them Use Crutches," *New York Times,* December 27, 2003.

5

United Kingdom

Alex Beer

The main types of pension provision in the UK are contributory state pensions, other state benefits paid to pensioners, and occupational and personal pensions.

State Pensions and Pensioner Benefits

State spending on pensioners is in the form of contributory state pensions and other state benefits paid to pensioners.

Contributory state pensions are funded on a pay-as-you-go basis from National Insurance contributions. Workers and employers pay National Insurance contributions, which also pay for some unemployment, disability, and bereavement benefits and for the National Health Service.

Contributory state pensions have two elements; both are compulsory for workers earning above a certain level. First is the basic State Pension, a flat-rate pension to which entitlement is determined by years of contributions credited. Second is a more earnings-related element: workers must either participate in the State Second Pension or a "contracted-out" equivalent, though people out of work may be credited with entitlement.

Employees' work status and whether they are contracted in to the State Second Pension determine the amount of their contributions to the state pensions. Self-employed workers, for example, pay a lower rate of contributions. Contracted-in employees, however, will pay 11 percent of their salary between the primary threshold (£94 a week in 2005–2006) and the upper earnings limit (£630 a week in 2005–2006), and 1 percent beyond. Their employers will pay 12.8 percent of each employee's salary above the secondary threshold, set at the same level as the primary threshold of £94 per week.

The state pension is currently payable at age 65 for men and age 60 for women, but this will equalize at age 65 between 2010 and 2020. Pensioners may defer receipt of the state pension, at a rate that is more than actuarially fair.[1]

For a variety of reasons, some people do not manage to achieve a state pension or a private pension that is above a level set by Parliament. If they do not have other provision for retirement, the government will step in with income-related assistance: the Pension Credit. Many other benefits are also available for pensioners, including Winter Fuel Payments of £200 for all households that include someone age 60 or older. Pensioners on low incomes can also get help with housing costs and toward local taxes (the Housing Benefit and Council Tax Benefit). Further benefits are available for people with disabilities or with caring responsibilities.

Basic State Pension

The maximum amount of basic State Pension is £82.05 a week (2005–2006). Receipt is based on a person's National Insurance contribution history.[2]

At present, a man will receive a full basic State Pension after making contributions or being treated as if he had made contributions for 44 of the years between the ages of 16 and 65. A man without a full contribution record will receive a partial reward. However, if his contributions would give him a pension of less than 25 percent of the full amount, then he will receive nothing. As the state pension age for women is 60, a woman need only make contributions for 39 years to receive a full pension. Once state pension age is equalized at 65, both men and women will need 44 years to receive a full pension.

To mitigate the effects of a broken work record on pension entitlement, a range of credits is available for those who did not have earnings in a specific week. Credits can be granted, for example, to those earning more than the lower earnings limit (£82 a week in 2005–2006) but less than the primary threshold (£94 a week in 2005–2006) at which they must start paying contributions. Credits are also received by the unemployed, by people claiming certain contributory benefits, or by men age 60 to 64.

In addition to credits, Home Responsibilities Protection is available to those who are not working because of caring responsibilities for children or the long-term sick or disabled. Home Responsibilities Protection does not credit the recipient with contributory years but instead reduces the number of years needed to receive a full pension—although for a full basic State Pension, the number of years cannot be reduced below 20.

Law requires that basic State Pension payments increase in line with prices, although recent years have also seen occasional increases greater than the level of inflation. For the rest of this Parliament,[3] the government has committed to increasing basic State Pension payments either by prices or by 2.5 percent a year, whichever is greater.

State Second Pension and Contracting Out

The UK has had a mandatory second-tier earnings-related pension system for employees (excluding the self-employed) since 1978. The system requires all employees either to be members of the State Second Pension, previously the State Earnings-Related Pension Scheme (SERPS), or to make equivalent savings in a contracted-out funded pension.

The State Second Pension was introduced in 2002, replacing SERPS, which came into effect in 1978. The SERPS regime changed a number of times between 1978 and 2002; therefore, the amount of each pensioner's payment will depend on the year he or she began contributing.

Entitlement to the state second-tier element is determined by earnings and associated accrual rates (the rate at which pensions are earned within different income brackets). Originally SERPS provided a 25 percent accrual rate for earnings between the lower earnings limit and the upper earnings limit. The rate was later reduced to 20 percent. The State Second Pension has added additional thresholds and accrual rates to make it more redistributive. Between the lower earnings limit and lower earnings threshold (£233 a week in 2005–2006), employees are treated as if they are earning at the lower earnings threshold, with an accrual rate of 40 percent on earnings between the two limits. The accrual rate on earnings above the lower earnings threshold and the upper earnings threshold (£535 a week in 2005–2006) is 10 percent. Beyond the upper earnings threshold to the upper earnings limit, accrual reverts to 20 percent.

In addition to treating workers with earnings between the lower earnings limit and the lower earnings threshold as if they earn at the lower earnings threshold, the State Second Pension gives credits to certain groups who do not have earnings. These groups, including some disabled people and carers (including carers of children younger than 6), are treated as if they are earning at the lower earnings threshold.

Second-tier state pension income is indexed to inflation. The amount of income people receive is determined by the various regimes to which they have been subject, and by the indexation of the various earnings thresholds. Current indicative plans are that the lower earnings limit and the upper earnings limit will only rise with prices, and thus fall relative to average earnings. But the lower earnings threshold is linked to earnings, which means that an increasing band of income will be deemed to be earnings at the level of the lower earnings threshold. As a result, the accrual system will become more flat rate.

If employees contract out of the state second tier, they and their employers must make equivalent contributions to funded pension schemes. Also, both employers and employees receive a rebate of National Insurance contributions. In 2003–2004, some 11 million people (47 percent of people with second-tier coverage) had coverage principally through contracted-out pension schemes.

In a significant proportion of cases, employees are automatically contracted out when they choose to join their occupational pension schemes. At least half of all salary-related occupational pension schemes are contracted out, as are 13 percent of defined contribution occupational pension schemes. It is also possible to contract out into an approved personal pension scheme.

The contracted-out rebate is set by the Government Actuary's Department to ensure that the contracted-out pension will secure equivalent benefits, given reasonable assumptions about rates of return and costs of investing.[4] Rates are generally reviewed every five years.

Pension Credit

Pension Credit, a major tool in tackling pensioner poverty, is a means-tested benefit available to people age 60 and older with low and moderate incomes. It has two elements: the Guarantee Credit and the Savings Credit. The latter is only available to people age 65 and older. These two components add up to a benefit that tops income up to a set level, currently

£109.45 a week (2005–2006) for a single pensioner, and is then tapered away at 40 pence for every extra pound of prebenefit income, up to a maximum income level of £105.55.

The government has pledged that the Guarantee Credit element will be indexed to earnings for the remainder of this Parliament. Beyond 2009, the rate at which Pension Credit will be indexed is undetermined.

Occupational and Personal Pensions

Private pensions are either occupational pension schemes, which are established by employers or groups of employers for their employees, or personal pension schemes, which are established by financial institutions (principally insurance companies) and are open to most people in the United Kingdom. Employers may also offer group personal pension arrangements for their employees. These are administered under personal pension rules, rather than occupational pension rules. Pensions paid under such schemes supplement pensions paid under the state pension scheme and, in many cases, replace the earnings-related elements of the state scheme.[5]

Private pension saving, providing the scheme meets strict conditions,[6] is tax privileged. Saving is out of pretax income, returns are tax free, and a tax-free lump sum of up to 25 percent of the value of the pension investment is available at retirement. The remaining income must be taken in the form of an annuity;[7] annuity income is subject to income tax.

Stakeholder pensions are a form of personal pension, introduced by the government in 2001 as a low-cost pension-saving product. Charges are capped at 1.5 percent of fund value per year for the first 10 years, then reduced to 1 percent. Stakeholder pensions bought prior to April 2005 have charges capped at 1 percent of fund value per year.

Pension Sustainability and Adequacy

The adequacy of future pensioner incomes is at risk. Although the UK pension system today is delivering better average retirement incomes than any previous generation has enjoyed (Department for Work and Pensions 2005), trends in future state and private pension provision imply that pension saving is falling, rather than rising to meet the demographic challenge (Pensions Commission 2004).

Today's Pensioners

For today's pensioners, the situation is far from bleak. The generation of pensioners currently retiring is seeing the benefits from when the SERPS accrual rate was at its highest, and from generous final salary pensions.

However, improvements in pensioner income were unequally distributed. Median incomes of the poorest fifth of pensioner couples lagged behind during the 1980s and 1990s, growing by only 34 percent from 1979 to 1996–1997, while those of the richest fifth grew by over 80 percent (Department for Work and Pensions 2005).

Since 1997, the government has targeted resources at improving outcomes for lower-income pensioners. The introduction of Pension Credit ensures that no pensioner has to live on less than £109 a week (in 2005–2006). Since 1997, absolute pensioner poverty has decreased by two-thirds.[8]

The UK has also highlighted how its macroeconomic stability, having enabled a stable low-inflation environment, is protecting nonindexed pensioner incomes and providing employment opportunities for all who want to work (Department for Work and Pensions 2005). And the economic outlook looks sustainable, despite an aging population (Her Majesty's Treasury 2005).

State Spending on Pensioners

In part, this sustainability is due to the stability of state spending on pensioners. In the 1980s and 1990s, reforms to the state pension system focused on decreasing costs. Earnings indexation of the basic State Pension was replaced by price indexation, the state pension age for women was increased (although this does not come into effect until 2010), and the SERPS accrual rate was reduced. Therefore, despite a near doubling of the pensioner population between now and 2050, state spending on pensioners[9] as a proportion of gross domestic product (GDP) will only increase from 5.1 percent of GDP to 6.7 percent of GDP in 2055–2056.[10]

Part of the increased expenditure results from higher spending on Pension Credit, since if current earnings indexation of Pension Credit continues, more of the pensioner population will become eligible. This potential spread makes it difficult for lower- to middle-income households to know how much state income they will receive in retirement. This may affect incentives to save.

Private Pension Participation

Occupational pension participation is in decline. In 1967, occupational pension membership peaked at 12.2 million. Today there are only 9.8 million members (National Statistics 2005). Membership declined steadily through the 1970s and 1980s, and pension policy in the 1980s and 1990s focused on promoting personal pensions. However, the availability of personal pensions has not stopped recent declines in private pension participation. Public confidence in occupational and personal pensions has been badly dented by mis-selling[11] and pension scandals. Employers' contributions have also decreased, as financial pressure on defined benefit schemes has increased (Pensions Commission 2004).

Abating the full impact of this decline is the increase in second-tier participation (State Second Pension and contracted-out participation), from 18 million in 1978–1979 to 26 million in 2003–2004. This is due to the extension of the State Second Pension to include almost 4 million carers and disabled people and nearly 6 million low and moderate earners (Department for Work and Pensions 2004b). However, as previously mentioned, state spending per pensioner is forecasted to fall.

In 2001, stakeholder pensions (low-cost personal pensions) were introduced. Originally charges were capped at 1 percent of the fund per year, although they have recently increased to 1.5 percent of the fund for the first 10 years and 1 percent thereafter. Stakeholder pensions have driven down charges across the personal pension market and increased pension coverage dramatically, with the requirement that employers having five or more employees and no suitable alternative pension provision identify a stakeholder pension scheme for their employees. In 2000, only 29 percent of organizations provided access to a pension. By 2004, 52 percent of organizations, covering 92 percent of employees, provided some type of pension access (National Statistics 2005).

However, there has not been a marked change in private pension participation[12]—the majority of employer stakeholder pension schemes are "empty shells" (Department for Work and Pensions 2004a). This may be explained by a lack of any incentive for employees to join (employers are not required to provide any contribution), or by inertia, or by reluctance or inability on the part of employees to decrease their current incomes.

Employment of Older Workers

Further decreasing participation in pensions is the low employment rate of workers over 50. Despite recent improvements in the over-50 employment rate, there is still a long way to go, particularly as increasing longevity has people spending much larger proportions of their life in retirement. Early retirement is by no means the greatest explanatory factor—these are disability and caring responsibilities (Department for Work and Pensions 2003). The ability to work for longer can have a significant impact on retirement income.

Undersaving

Given these trends, the government has estimated that 3 million people may be seriously undersaving for their retirement, and a further 5 to 10 million more may need to save more or work longer (Department for Work and Pensions 2002). Otherwise, a significant proportion of today's workers will not build up the retirement income they might expect.

Pension Reform

In recognition of the challenges that the UK's aging population brings, the government established an independent commission to review the regime for private pensions and long-term savings.[13]

In the meantime, the government introduced legislation to simplify and restore some confidence in private pensions. The Finance Act 2004 swept away eight separate regimes for tax-privileged pension saving and replaced them with one flexible regime based on a lifetime limit of £1.5 million (in 2006) of tax-privileged pension saving. The Pensions Act 2004 strengthened pension regulation and protection, replacing the Occupational Pensions Regulatory Authority with a more proactive Pensions Regulator, and establishing the Pension Protection Fund. The Pension Protection Fund is a new public body that protects members of defined benefit schemes by paying compensation if their employer benefit becomes insolvent and the pension scheme is underfunded.

First Report of the Pensions Commission

In October 2004, the Pensions Commission published their first report,[14] which analyzed current and projected pension trends and set out the stark choices facing the UK. People must accept a society with relatively poorer pensioners, or save more, or work longer, or pay a higher proportion of taxes to pensioners.

Government's Pension Principles

In February 2005, the government set out principles against which to measure proposed reform of the pension system (Department for Work and Pensions 2005).

- Reform should promote personal responsibility, providing the right incentives to work and save.
- Reform should be fair, protecting the poorest, women, and carers, and rewarding those who have saved.
- Reform should be affordable, meeting expectations while keeping government spending sustainable, to ensure economic stability and productivity.
- Reform should be simple, so that people understand the system, enabling them to make informed choices.
- Reform should also be sustainable, in the belief that successful provision for retirement involves a wide range of stakeholders working together: the financial services industry, trade unions, advisors, individuals, government, and opposition parties must all play their part in creating a stable environment.

Second Report of the Pensions Commission

In November 2005, the Pensions Commission published their recommendations for the UK pension system (Pensions Commission 2005). Their key recommendations included proposals for both the state and private pension systems. Proposed measures would extend pension coverage and participation (as well as increase the basic State Pension and decrease reliance on means testing) by indexing the basic State Pension to wages from 2010, and by gradually increasing the state pension age.

A National Pension Saving Scheme

The commission proposed establishing a low-cost National Pension Savings Scheme and applying the principle of automatic enrollment nationally. Employees not covered by other adequate pension arrangements would be automatically enrolled into the scheme, but with the right to opt out. The commission recommended that a modest matching contribution by employers be compulsory.

The scheme would overcome inertia toward pension saving. It would aim to ensure sufficient incomes in retirement with 4 percent of contributions from individual post-tax earnings, 3 percent mandatory matching contributions from the employer, and 1 percent in either tax relief or tax credits from the government. These levels of saving would push people beyond the threshold for means-tested benefits and beyond the savings disincentives associated with them.

Reforming the State System

The commission proposed reforms to make the state pension system more understandable and less means tested. Their recommendations included phasing out the earnings-related component of the State Second Pension,[15] gradually eliminating contracting out, and making future accruals to the basic State Pension universal rather than contributory. In the longer term, they proposed that the value of the basic State Pension be indexed to earnings, thus increasing guaranteed pension income from the state and reducing reliance on means testing.

Also recommended was a gradual long-term increase in state pension age, proportionate to life expectancy, to offset the increased expenditure that would result from restoring the basic State Pension's link to earnings. This proposal would raise state pension age to 66 by about 2030 and to 67 by 2050.

Responses to Reform

The government welcomed the Pensions Commission's recommendations and weighed them against the tests outlined for reform proposals. Before ruling any proposals in or out, the government also attempted to assess public consensus during a national debate that culminated in a

National Pensions Day on March 18, 2006.[16] By actively reaching out to workers, pensioners, and other stakeholders, the government hoped to discover where consensus lay.

The national debate revealed widespread agreement that there is a "pensions problem," and all but the general public seemed to agree that the state pension age must increase. However, no consensus emerged on what the complete reform should look like.

The Conservative Party called on the government to seriously consider the Pension Commission's proposals. The media and older people's charities welcomed the proposals. Private pension providers and business leaders agreed in principle with the need to strengthen the state system and decrease reliance on means testing. The Trades Union Congress contended that compulsory saving in funded pensions was the best way to ensure adequate pension saving.

The majority of these organizations have actively engaged in the pension debate. Pension providers and insurance companies have risen to the challenge set by the government, to formulate a workable model for a national pension-saving scheme. The government published its intentions for reform in May 2006. However, public response has been more difficult to gauge. Those aggrieved have the greater tendency to speak out, and complaints of being made to work longer and of pension inadequacy, without any recognition that reform is tough, have dominated the Have Your Say section of the BBC News web site.[17]

Conclusion

The appetite for UK pension reform is driven by concerns about the adequacy of future pensioner incomes rather than by any impending fiscal crisis. Crisis has been averted by price indexing state pensions and targeting state pensioner benefits on the poorest. However, projected decreases in state spending per pensioner as a proportion of GDP will not likely be met by increased private provision. Current projections imply that future pensioners will be poorer relative to average earnings.

The Pensions Commission recommendations address this issue with proposals to shore up the state pension system and increase private pension saving through automatic enrollment into a national system of personal accounts, with mandatory contributions from employers.

The government welcomed the Pension Commission's proposals and listened to other stakeholders during its national pension debate. There was widespread agreement that the system has problems, but no clear consensus on the solution. In May 2006, the government published the reforms it intended to take forward.

Postscript

The government of the United Kingdom submitted its Pensions Bill to Parliament on November 28, 2006.[18] The bill aims for long-term pension reform through a fairer, more generous state pension and private saving (Department for Work and Pensions 2006b). Private saving is to be facilitated by a new national system of low-cost personal accounts (Department for Work and Pensions 2006a). Key reform proposals are summarized below.

State Pensions

- The state pension age will rise gradually, from 65 to 66 from 2024, to 67 from 2034, and to 68 from 2044.
- Probably from 2012, the basic state pension will be indexed in line with average earnings, rather than with inflation, subject to affordability and the fiscal position. The precise date will be announced at the beginning of the next Parliament.

Personal Savings Accounts

- A new system of personal savings accounts will be crafted, into which workers without existing pension coverage will be automatically enrolled.
- Employers will make a compulsory contribution of 3 percent of salary to the plan, with employees paying 4 percent and the government, 1 percent.
- A delivery authority will be created to design and establish personal accounts.
- The employer contribution will be phased in over three years, and the government will consider a longer phasing-in period for smaller businesses.

- Self-employed and unemployed individuals will be able to join the scheme voluntarily; saving would be at the individual's discretion and would not be compulsory in any way.

Help for Women and Carers

- The number of years of contributions needed to qualify for a full state pension will be reduced to 30 years for both men and women (it is currently 39 for women and 44 for men).
- Measures will be introduced to enable people caring for children or the disabled to build up an entitlement to the state pension without having to make a minimum level of contributions.
- This should mean that 70 percent of women will be eligible for a full basic state pension by 2010, as opposed to the 30 percent eligible now.

Other Changes

- The current system of contracting out from the State Second Pension will be abolished for defined contribution pension plans.
- The State Second Pension will evolve into a flat-rate top-up pension by 2030.

NOTES

1. There are two state pension deferral options, and the amount received depends on how long claiming is deferred: (1) extra weekly state pension payments increased by 10.4 percent for each year of deferral; or (2) a one-off taxable lump sum equal to the value of the state pension deferred, plus annual interest of 2 percent above the base rate and then the normal weekly state pension.

2. There are also spousal additions to the basic State Pension, up to 60 percent of the pensioner's entitlement, granted when spouses or civil partners have not made sufficient contributions of their own. Survivor pensions are also paid.

3. The current Parliament convened in 2005 and will end its term in 2009.

4. See http://www.gad.gov.uk/pensions/contracting_out.htm for more details.

5. That is to say, they are contracted-out pension schemes. Pension schemes can only be contracted-out schemes if Her Majesty's Revenue and Customs are satisfied the scheme meets relevant conditions (see http://www.hmrc.gov.uk for more details).

6. More detail on these restrictions is available on http://www.hmrc.gov.uk.

7. Except in very limited cases; in these, very cautious income draw-down is monitored.

8. Poverty was measured as 60 percent of median income in 1996–1997 (Department for Work and Pensions 2005).

9. State spending on pensioners includes state pensions, Pension Credit, Winter Fuel, and other pensioner-specific benefits. It does not include all benefits to which pensioners are entitled. However, the picture remains the same.

10. Department for Work and Pensions, benefit expenditure tables, December 2006, http://www.dwp.gov.uk/asd/asd4/long_term.asp.

11. *Mis-selling* most frequently refers to incorrectly advising people to start a personal pension at the expense of leaving their occupational pension—and thus missing out on employer contributions.

12. In 1999–2000, private pension schemes had 14.6 million members (around 46 percent of the working-age population). In 2003–2004, they had 14.3 million members (44 percent of the working-age population) (Department for Work and Pensions, Family Resources Survey, 2006, http://www.dwp.gov.uk/asd/frs/).

13. The commission was composed of three members chosen for their expertise and experience. The chair of the commission is Adair Turner.

14. *Pensions: Challenges and Choices.*

15. State Second Pension entitlement and contracted-out rebates are determined in part by the upper earnings limit. The commission's proposal to freeze this limit will result, over time, in the state second pension becoming flat rate and contracted-out rebates shrinking, leading to the gradual disappearance of contracting out (by around 2030).

16. See http://www.dwp.gov.uk/debate/index.asp for more details.

17. See http://newsforums.bbc.co.uk/nol/thread.jspa?threadID=444&&&edition=2&ttl=20060222164702.

18. See http://www.publications.parliament.uk/pa/pabills/200607/pensions.htm.

REFERENCES

Department for Work and Pensions. 2002. *Simplicity, Security and Choice: Working and Saving for Retirement.* London: Department for Work and Pensions, December.

———. 2003. *Factors Affecting the Labour Market Participation of Older Workers.* Research Report 200. London: Department for Work and Pensions, November.

———. 2004a. *Employers' Pension Provision Survey 2003.* Research Report 207. London: Department for Work and Pensions, March.

———. 2004b. *Second-Tier Pension Provision 1978/9-2003/04.* London: Department for Work and Pensions, January.

———. 2005. *Principles for Reform: The National Pensions Debate.* London: Department for Work and Pensions, February.

———. 2006a. *Personal Accounts: A New Way to Save.* London: Department for Work and Pensions, December. http://www.dwp.gov.uk/pensionsreform/new_way.asp. (Accessed April 18, 2007.)

———. 2006b. *Security in Retirement: Towards a New Pension System*. London: Department for Work and Pensions, May. http://www.dwp.gov.uk/pensionsreform/whitepaper. asp. (Accessed April 18, 2007.)

Her Majesty's Treasury. 2005. *Long-Term Public Finance Report: An Analysis of Fiscal Sustainability*. London: Her Majesty's Treasury, December.

National Statistics. 2005. *Pension Trends*. Newport, UK: Office for National Statistics.

Pensions Commission. 2004. *Pensions: Challenges and Choices. The First Report of the Pensions Commission*. London: The Stationery Office, October.

———. 2005. *A New Pension Settlement for the Twenty-First Century: The Second Report of the Pensions Commission*. London: The Stationery Office, November.

John Turner

The United Kingdom is a major innovator in retirement income policy. I will discuss three innovative aspects of UK retirement income policy covered by Alex Beer: privatizing social security using voluntary carve-out individual accounts, extending private pension coverage by using greater degrees of compulsion on workers and employers, and raising the social security early retirement age to 65.

The United Kingdom is the only high-income country using voluntary carve-out individual accounts—the type proposed by President George W. Bush. (Japan has voluntary carve-out accounts, but it uses defined benefit plans for those accounts.) With voluntary carve-out accounts, participation in the earnings-related part of social security is not compulsory, but workers who opt out must participate in alternative arrangements.

A number of individual account myths are part of the U.S. Social Security debate. In traditional economics, expanded choice is always viewed as desirable. In that framework, having voluntary carve-out accounts would enhance Americans' well-being because it would expand their range of choices. Instead of facing a Social Security monopoly, people could choose a form of retirement income provision that better matches their preferences.

The UK experience demonstrates why expanded choice in the retirement income system is not always desirable. Due to a lack of financial sophistication, many UK workers have been made worse off by taking the voluntary carve-out accounts. Beer mentioned the mis-selling scandal, in which those selling investments in individual accounts provided false information. While that scandal is well known among U.S. pension experts, what is not appreciated is the magnitude of the errors made. Thirteen billion pounds has been paid to the victims of mis-selling. Even though that is a large amount of money in the context of the U.S. economy—about $26 billion—keep in mind that the UK's economy is a sixth the size of the U.S.'s economy.

A fundamental problem with voluntary carve-out accounts is that it is difficult to set the tradeoff in benefit levels between full social security and reduced social security benefits plus an individual account. If workers are treated generously, the accounts become expensive for the government in that payroll taxes are reduced with little reduction in social security benefits. However, if workers moving to the voluntary accounts are not treated generously, then they may have made a mistake.

The UK has had problems setting the terms of the benefits tradeoff. The UK Government Actuary's Department resets the rebate that goes to the accounts every five years. Recently, two large insurance companies have advised their clients not to participate in the voluntary carve-out accounts, believing an error was made in setting the rebate. When the rebate was set, interest rates were quite low. The Government Actuary's Department thought interest rates were going to rise, and they set the rebate accordingly. But the interest rate did not rise, and so the rebate was not sufficient for people who took those accounts.

The idea of voluntary carve-out accounts is now being rejected by workers in the United Kingdom. It is ironic that such accounts are being proposed for the United States. The number of individual account holders has declined by about 40 percent since the early 1990s—despite the growth of the labor force. And the Pensions Commission has recommended phasing out the voluntary carve-out accounts as part of social security.

My second point is about extending coverage provided by private pensions, using greater degrees of compulsion. In the UK, employers are not required to provide a pension plan. However, employers with five or more employees not offering a plan are required to designate a pension provider to which employees can contribute. Thus, the employer is required to have a payroll deduction facility for employees wanting to contribute to an individual retirement account. The idea is to make it easier for workers to participate, because they can do so through a payroll deduction instead of having to make the contribution on their own.

The policy has not been in effect for very long—only a year or two. But noncompliance has been widespread; many employers, particularly small employers, required to offer such plans are not doing so. Employers are required to set up a plan with a financial service provider, so there is a cost to employers, even though they do not have to make contributions on behalf of their employees. I assume that the compliance issue will eventually be resolved, but it has not been adequately addressed so far. More importantly, few workers have adopted the plans. The majority of employers that have offered them have no participants.

The Pensions Commission is taking compulsion a degree further. Their proposal would require employers not only to offer a pension, but to automatically enroll their workers and to make a matching contribution for their employees. Employees could opt out if they wanted to. If they did not opt out, they would be required to contribute. This policy is one step short of mandating that the worker participate in the pension.

The third policy issue is the pensionable age, which is the earliest age that social security benefits can be received. It will be raised to 65 for UK women by 2020, and it is that age already for UK men. In comparison, the pensionable age is 62 in the United States, 61 in Sweden, and 60 in Canada. So 65 is significantly higher than in many other high-income countries, though Ireland and some others have set the pensionable age at 65.

When the pensionable age is high, do most people actually work until that age? The answer is no, they do not. In countries with a pensionable age of 65, alternative ways of retiring have developed. Many people take disability benefits at a younger age. Workers can take employer-provided benefits at earlier ages. Interestingly, workers can take a pension benefit earlier if they have contracted out (at age 60) than if they had not contracted out. Labor force participation for persons aged 55 to 64 is actually slightly lower in the United Kingdom than in the United States.

With increasing longevity, only three options exist for social security reform within the traditional system, all of them unpleasant—reducing old-age benefits, raising taxes, or raising the age at which benefits can be received. Nicholas Barr, a distinguished economist at the London School of Economics, has recently stated that the central problem of pension finance is the age at which people are first eligible to claim their pensions (Barr 2006). He seems to have influenced the UK Pensions Commission: it has proposed that the pensionable age be indexed to life expectancy, so that a constant proportion of adult life would be spent in retirement.

Indexing social security to life expectancy may seem like a logical extension of price indexing, but it is actually a radical proposal—the UK would be the first country to index the earliest age at which you can receive benefits to life expectancy. Other countries have indexed benefits to life expectancy, and Sweden is an example. But no country has indexed the early retirement age to increases in life expectancy.

In summary, the United Kingdom is the only country that has voluntary carve-out accounts, that is, individual accounts of the type that President Bush has proposed, but they are considering phasing out these accounts. Whether they decide to phase them out, workers are not choosing them to the extent they used to. The UK has a short but largely unsuccessful experience with mandatory universal individual retirement accounts. The essential problem is that people who have been offered these accounts have not participated without there being an employer match. Last, the UK has a relatively high pensionable age of 65 and has proposed indexing that age to improvements in life expectancy so that it could reach age 67 by 2050. We can gain useful insights from the experience of the United Kingdom as to how these reforms might work in practice in the United States.

REFERENCE

Barr, Nicholas. 2006. "Non-Financial Defined Contribution Pensions: Mapping the Terrain." In *Pension Reform: Issues and Prospects for Non-Financial Defined Contribution Schemes,* edited by Robert Holzmann and Edward Palmer (57–69). Washington, DC: World Bank Publications.

COMMENTARY

Stanford G. Ross

Examining social security reform in other countries is a good idea, because it is not only important to keep talking about Social Security reform in the United States, but to find new ways to get people to think about it. Every country under review in this volume may be seen as making a tradeoff between social protection concerns and fiscal burdens. The issue is how to strike an appropriate balance.

Many of the continental European countries, like Germany and France, appear to be at one extreme since they have the largest fiscal costs and maintain the greatest amount of social protection. It is doubtful they have achieved an appropriate balance for the long term. The UK may be seen as at the other end of the spectrum. It has done the best job of constraining fiscal costs, but it has basically lost a fundamental core of reliable social protection. We cannot read Alex Beer's paper and analyze the Pension Commission's report without seeing that the UK does not have a basic core benefit that supports the needs of a highly diverse country. The U.S. is somewhere in the middle. Its fiscal costs are only modestly excessive by OECD standards, and it still maintains a strong measure of social protection. Our average replacement rate is somewhere between 35 and 40 percent. It is not huge, but given America's size and diversity, it is a good measure of protection, particularly because lower-income people tend to have higher replacement rates while higher-income people have lower rates.

I was struck by how timid the UK's response to its dilemma seems. Tony Blair's government had shown it could be aggressive at times, but it surely was not aggressive in attacking this issue. Creating a commission strung out the debate, and now their consultations will provoke further delays. And even with the commission's report, the word "timid" is a good characterization of its recommendations. Given the UK's social welfare traditions, its inability to establish a tax-based pension system of even modest proportions, like that in the U.S., strikes me as quite remarkable. The commission's recommendations continue to reflect the second-best solution of trying to use tax incentives to create still another optional individual account system.

So what lesson do we draw from that? Perhaps an OECD country today cannot accept increasing fiscal costs for social protection in a highly competitive global economy. It also suggests that if this is so, a country should be very careful in its reforms, so as not to reduce fundamental social protections too much or too fast or incoherently. I believe that is exactly what the United Kingdom has done. It has left itself with a lot of people who have very low pensions. The UK may need even more means testing, but they already have more means testing and income-related supplements than would be acceptable in the United States.

However, I admire much about the UK's system. In particular, they do furnish retirees with affordable health care—the UK is way ahead of the U.S. on this score. And perhaps that is why the UK can get away with inadequate pensions. One thing that may inhibit U.S. Social Security reform is the growing cost of our health care system. And the recent so-called Medicare modernization reforms seem to me not to be a solution. They seem just to be exacerbating the problem, which is that the public is going to be concerned about any attempt to erode basic pension benefits when they anticipate high health care costs in old age.

The United Kingdom supplies a cautionary tale that advocates of voluntary individual accounts for the United States have yet to adequately address. The U.S. voluntary private and individual account systems are quite substantial. They do provide useful supplements while the public-financed Social Security system continues to deliver a basic core of pension support that people can rely on. So if American corporations continue forgoing retiree pensions for defined contribution plans, like 401(k)s, while providing less retiree health care, the present Social Security system will extend basic protection. But if we ever lose our basic Social Security system, then I think changes in our voluntary supplements will cause much more concern.

I suppose, the U.S. and the UK are unique, as are France, Germany, Japan, and all other OECD countries. In every country, the political system works in a distinctive way. Whether their pension systems offer what people need is hard to say. In the end, a democracy produces what the citizens vote for. However, these problems may take time to be worked out responsibly, as the case studies in this volume show. From my standpoint, the present stalemate in the United States is a far better situation in the short term than ill-advised change would be. Ultimately, the U.S. must improve the social protection efficiency and financial sustainability of its public pension system, but it should be able to do this without seriously eroding the basic level of social protection the system now provides. Some modest changes, particularly on the revenue side and in the retirement age in the long term, could get the job done, as I testified before the Senate Finance Committee in 2005.[1] I remain an optimist on U.S. pension matters.

NOTE

1. "Social Security: Achieving Sustainable Solvency," hearing before the Committee on Finance, United States Senate, 109th Congress, First Session, May 25, 2005. http://finance.senate.gov/hearings/27402.pdf. (Accessed February 20, 2007.)

6

Italy

Alicia Puente Cackley, Tom Moscovitch,
and Benjamin Pfeiffer

M any countries, including the United States, are grappling with demographic change and its effect on their national pension systems and long-term fiscal posture. With increasing longevity and declining birthrates, the number of workers for each retiree is falling in most developed countries. These trends can strain the finances of national pension programs, particularly those in which contributions from current workers fund payments to current beneficiaries—a form of financing known as pay-as-you-go.

Demographic and economic challenges are less severe in the United States than in many other developed countries—the birthrate is not as low, people are more likely to stay in the labor force for a greater number of years, and immigration continues to provide young workers. Yet projections show that the Social Security program faces a significant long-term financing problem. Because some countries have already undertaken national pension reform to address demographic changes similar to those occurring in the United States, their experiences can provide lessons for U.S. policymakers.

Italy is facing a demographic challenge substantially greater than that of the U.S.; greater, indeed, than the average for all the countries of the European Union. (See figure 6.1 below.) By considering the reforms Italy has put into place, as well as the process by which they were achieved, U.S. policymakers may be able to draw some conclusions about the difficulties to expect as they consider their own reform plans.

Figure 6.1. Projected Economic Old-Age Dependency Ratios, U.S. and European Union Countries

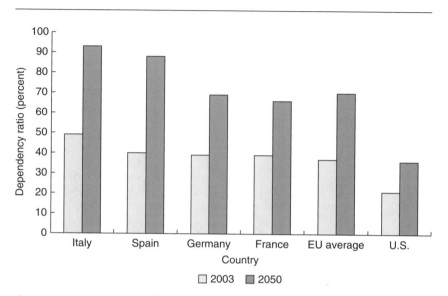

Sources: European Commission, Economic Policy Committee (2001) and Toossi (2002).

Notes: The old-age dependency ratio is represented by the total inactive population as a percentage of the employed population ages 15 to 64. U.S. figures are based on the authors' calculations using Bureau of Labor Statistics labor force and population projections for U.S. residents ages 65 and older and ages 16 to 64 for 2000, 2010, and 2050.

Italy's Pension System Before 1992

The Italian pension system consists of three pillars: (1) mandatory old-age insurance (MOA), which also provides survivor insurance and disability benefits;[1] (2) supplementary pension systems, including closed-end funds formed by employers or employees, and collective pension funds, which are mostly funded and voluntary (Pollnerová 2002); and (3) private insurance annuities or individual accounts. Supplementary pensions and private insurance substitute for the MOA in only a few cases. They are generally not mandated and they are funded by individual contributions (OECD 2004).

Prior to 1992, funding for MOA was from a payroll tax of 26.4 percent (one-third paid by employees, two-thirds, by employers). However, the state made up any shortfall between revenue and outlays; in 1992, government estimates indicated that payroll taxes would have to rise to between 35 percent and 42 percent to fully fund the system (Brugiavini and Galasso 2003).

MOA was available to men age 60 and older and women age 55 and older who had contributed to the pension system for at least 15 years. However, an early retirement option allowed private-sector workers to claim benefits at any age after 35 years of contributions. Public-sector workers could claim benefits after 20 years of tax contributions for men and 15 years for women. The pension benefit was based on final salary (the average of the last five years of real earnings for private-sector workers and final salary for public-sector workers) and years of service. Years of service, up to a maximum of 40, were multiplied by a factor of 2 percent and applied to the final salary. Thus, the maximum benefit replaced 80 percent of earnings. Benefits were indexed to nominal wage growth. Perhaps most importantly, no actuarial penalty was assessed on early retirees.

In addition to the public pension program, Italian workers receive a severance payment called the *Trattmento Fine Rapporto* (*TFR*), which for workers in the private sector is equal to the cumulative total of 7.41 percent of earnings in each year. This is paid by employers and retained in a fund that the employers manage directly. It is paid out as a lump sum at retirement and in the meantime, serves as a source of capital for the employer. For this reason, employees have an incentive to retire early, since they are not earning a very high rate of interest while the money remains in the fund—about 1 percentage point below current bond market interest rates.[2]

Italy also provides retirees a means-tested minimum pension (a maximum of about €6,300 per year for a single person in 2002) for people who contributed to MOA, with a supplement available for those age 70 or older. For Italians ineligible for the minimum pension, a social assistance program ensures that people receive minimum support of about €4,725 a year, which is also supplemented for those age 70 or older.

Recent Reforms and Their Budgetary Context

The Italian government has enacted several reforms of its public program since 1980, most notably in 1992 and 1995. Together, these reforms both reduced the cost of the program and increased contribution rates. Most significantly, while the system's funding is still pay-as-you-go, the calculation of benefits is now "contribution based," through notional defined contribution (NDC) accounts.

Italy's most recent pension reforms were undertaken at a time of serious budgetary problems. To enter the European Monetary Union, countries were required under the Maastricht Treaty of 1992 to comply with the following convergence criteria: (1) fiscal deficits generally below 3 percent of gross domestic product (GDP); (2) a public debt ratio not to exceed 60 percent;[3] (3) an inflation rate not more than 1.5 percentage points above the three best-performing member states; and (4) long-term interest rates not more than 2 percentage points above that of the three member states with the best price stability.[4] At the beginning of the 1990s, the ratio of deficit to GDP in Italy was 11.7 percent and the public debt to GDP ratio was 97.1 percent (Bosi, Giarda, and Onofri 2003).

The first significant reform measures are known as the 1992 Amato reforms, for the name of the then–prime minister. One goal of the reforms was to lay a foundation for an equitable, straightforward pension system, rather than to make painful spending cuts that would not be accepted by segments of the population. To this end, many of the changes were phased in over 10 years. Specifically, the reforms increased the state retirement age from 55 to 60 years for women and from 60 to 65 years for men, increased the number of years of contributions for eligibility to 20, changed from nominal wage to price indexation of benefits, and for younger workers, increased the number of years of contributions used to calculate retirement benefits from the last 5 years to workers' entire working life. Private- and public-sector employees' early retirement eligibility requirements were also brought more into balance, by raising the number of contribution years required of public-sector employees from 20 to 35. According to Italian researchers, these measures decreased public pension liabilities by at least 25 percent in projected net present value (Brugiavini and Galasso 2003). However, because they were phased in over time, and especially because there was still no actuarial adjustment for early retirement, they did not produce needed savings in the public-pension budget.

The second set of reforms, known as the 1995 Dini reforms, was an attempt to change the basic rules for granting benefits to future retirees, while at the same time injecting actuarial balance into the early retirement benefits. The Dini reforms also increased required contributions to the program to a total of 32.7 percent of covered wages (8.89 percent from employees and 23.81 percent from employers) (OECD 2000).[5] Specifically, the reforms mandated the creation of a notional defined contribution program similar to Sweden's.

Under Italy's NDC program, each employee has a notional public pension account credited with one-third of his gross wages each year. The account balance earns interest at a rate equal to a five-year moving average of growth in the country's GDP (OECD 2005). A worker may decide to retire as early as age 57, as long as his account is large enough to provide a minimum benefit of 1.2 times the social assistance benefit.[6] The increase in benefits for additional years of work during this period is designed to be actuarially level. The benefit is calculated based on the balance of the account, the age at retirement, and a factor that will be adjusted periodically based on changes in life expectancies at various ages. The benefits after retirement, which were linked to the legislated level of the minimum wage before 1992, are now linked partly to changes in prices. After the calculation of initial benefits, the portion of benefits below a specified level (equal to three times the minimum pension, or about two-thirds of average earnings) is increased based on the increase in prices. A portion of benefits above that level increases by 90 percent of the rate of price inflation. Benefits exceeding five times the minimum pension are increased by 75 percent of the rate of price inflation.

Key features of the 1992 Amato reform (see table 6.1), including retirement ages and the reference period for calculating the initial benefit, were phased in over 10 years. Italy's transition in 1995 to a NDC public pension system won't be complete until people who began working in 1996 or later have retired. Thus, those who contributed to the system since before 1992 could receive some of their benefits based on three different sets of rules (pre-1992, 1992–1995 and post-1995). The OECD projects that, once it is fully implemented, this program will replace an average of about 89 percent of net wages for most workers who retire at age 65 (OECD 2005).[7] The rate varies little by income level. In contrast, the Italian pension program in place before the 1995 reform provided benefits that replaced a higher portion of earnings for people with low earnings than for people with high earnings. The less-generous indexation of benefits under the new system, however, means that their purchasing power will fall for most retirees.

The Italian public pension program is expected to become financially solvent by 2050. Currently, however, general tax revenue is needed to cover shortfalls in the pension system's financing. Program expenditures are projected to rise from 14.4 percent of GDP in 2005 to 15.9 percent in

Table 6.1. Changes in Key Features of Italian Pensions During the 1990s

	Pre-1992 reform	1992–1995 reform	Post-1995 reform
Normal retirement age	60 (men) 55 (women)	65 (men) 60 (women)	Any age, starting at 57 (men and women)
Pensionable earnings	Average of last five years of real earnings	Career-average earnings	Career contributions (capitalized at an annual rate using a five-year moving average of past GDP growth rates)
Pension benefit	2% x pensionable earnings x years of tax payments ≤ 40	2% x pensionable earnings x years of tax payments ≤ 40	Proportional to accrued value of career contributions; proportionality factor increases with age up to 65[a]
Years of contributions needed for eligibility	15	20	5
Total payroll tax (employee and employer)	24.5% gross earnings	27.1% gross earnings	32.7% gross earnings

Source: Brugiavini and Peracchi (2004).

GDP = gross domestic product

a. The proportionality factor takes into account the average residual life expectancy at retirement based on 1990 life tables and a fixed real rate of return of 1.5 percent that reflects long-run forecasts of annual GDP growth.

2040, before dropping to 14.7 percent in 2050 (Dang, Antolin, and Oxley 2001). Some researchers have concluded that the reforms have had deleterious effects on the economy. The high level of contributions increases Italy's employment costs compared with other nations, which may retard economic growth. In addition, uncertainties created by the drawn-out timetable for implementing reforms encouraged some workers to retire early. In response to the 1992 reforms, Italians retired as soon as they were eligible in order to avoid the new provisions. The continued availability of severance pay packages, which in effect earn low rates of interest during employment, also encouraged early retirement.

The 2004 Pension Reform Act[8] gradually phases in restrictions that should reduce early retirements. Beginning in 2008, the minimum retirement age will be 60, provided that the worker has contributed to the program for at least 35 years. In 2010, the age will increase to 61 and in 2014, to 62.[9] However, a worker with 40 years of contributions may still retire at any age. With 20 years of contributions men may retire at 65, and women who began contributing before 1996 may retire at 60. Until 2014, women with at least 35 years of contributions may retire at age 57 as long as they accept additional reductions in benefits (Ministero 2004).

In November 2005, the Italian parliament voted to allow workers to redirect contributions from *TFRs* into private and occupational pension funds. The new law doesn't take effect until 2008 to allow companies more time to adapt to the new rules. The provision is expected to benefit the private pension industry in Italy, perhaps shifting as much as €13 billion per year into supplementary private and occupational pension plans (U.S. Social Security Administration 2005). It is also expected to strengthen the second pillar of the pension system in general.

Given the expected shortfalls in the program's finances over the next few decades, Italians continue to discuss the need for additional reform. Options under consideration include further increasing women's retirement age to men's age (65 years),[10] raising the minimum retirement age, increasing contribution rates, and increasing penalties for early retirement. Recent reforms have also focused on new incentives for private voluntary savings programs, such as the *TFR* legislation cited above.

The Impact of Italy's Budget Process and Political Climate on Pension Reform

The Italian budget process and the political climate during the 1990s both played a role in the public pension reforms. Early in the decade, reform of the public pension system was part of an overall government strategy of budgetary consolidation, precipitated most directly by the need to meet eligibility criteria set out in the Maastricht Treaty.

Italy's budget process is based on the rule that any new expenditure legislation must indicate the means of financing, known as the financial coverage rule. The process begins with an initial agreement between

Parliament and the executive branch on target balances of the state budget and the general government account. The executive branch then proposes two bills, one to cover the state budget for existing legislation and one to cover proposals for new legislation. Parliament may then offer amendments to these bills during its budget session, but may not change the originally agreed-upon budget balance. Thus, the government's budget decisions are constrained. The only way that the overall budget balance can change over time is if revenues or expenditures from past legislation change, or if the expected financial effects of new legislation turn out to be incorrect. In that case, midyear corrections are enacted to put the budget back on track (Pisauro 2003). The public pension system is considered to be part of the unified budget and therefore subject to the financial coverage rule. However, the Parliament in its budget session does not consider the specifics of the projected revenues and outlays from the program, but only the balance that is to be financed by the state (Pisauro 2003).

The design of each pension reform was significantly affected by the political climate at the time it was enacted. The 1992 Amato pension reforms were enacted during a time of fiscal imbalance in the public pension system. As a result, while both workers and retirees were affected by the subsequent reductions in net pension wealth, younger workers bore the brunt of the burden and in general the reforms were accepted as necessary. Subsequent pension reforms, however, have been viewed as more structural, and garnering political support for them is increasingly dependent on how costs are distributed across generations. The Dini reforms of 1995, for example, also fell most heavily on younger cohorts and were therefore more readily supported by the older voting population. However, in 1994 the Berlusconi government also proposed pension reform, including cuts in net pension wealth that were much more evenly distributed across all workers. These reforms were rejected by the voting public.

Conclusions

The Italian government has clearly made progress in its attempts to adjust the country's public pension system to meet the demographic realities of an aging population. While the long-term outlook is somewhat more hopeful, short-term imbalances are still problematic. Because the NDC plan only applies to workers entering the workforce after 1995, and many workers are still able to retire early (and indeed, still have incentives to do so), the benefits of the reforms are watered down. According to the European Commission's Economic Policy Committee, Italy's inactive population age 65 and older, as a percentage of the employed population age 15 to 64, will be 93 percent in 2050—the highest among the 25 countries (European Commission, Economic Policy Committee 2005). The implication is that even actuarially adjusted early retirement benefits may not be enough to encourage increased participation in the workforce and relieve stress on the system.

Another implication of the pension system reforms is that second-pillar growth has become essential to the long-term retirement prospects of younger workers, who will now receive lower replacement rates from the first-pillar system. Some progress appears to have been made in strengthening second-pillar growth, but it is too soon to tell what proportion of employees will take advantage of their new ability to move *TFR* contributions into private or occupational pension funds.

Finally, there is still a risk that over time early retirees may create political pressure for discretionary increases in pension benefits. All of these factors open the Italian pension system's long-term projections of balance to further questions and analysis.

NOTES

1. There is also a seniority pension not available to workers who entered the workforce after 1996. Workers still eligible for the seniority pension can receive it at age 57 with 35 years of contributions or at any age with 38 years of contributions (rising to 40 years of contributions by 2008). The seniority pension is calculated as a progressive percent (0.9 percent to 2 percent) of earnings multiplied times the number of years of earnings, up to a maximum of 40.

2. The *TFR* minimum rate of return is currently about 3.1 percent (1.5 percent plus 75 percent of the inflation rate, currently about 2.1 percent). This compares with corporate bond rates of about 4 percent.

3. A country with a higher debt-to-GDP ratio can nevertheless adopt the euro if its debt levels are falling steadily.

4. A fifth criteria concerns exchange-rate stability. The exchange rate should have stayed within defined fluctuation margins for two years. These margins are set by the European exchange-rate mechanism, an optional system for member states that want to link their currency to the euro.

5. In part, however, this resulted from relabeling several contributions under a single social security tax. Some employers, including those in economically distressed areas, are entitled to pay a lower contribution rate.

6. To be eligible at age 57, a retiree must have contributed for five years.

7. Currently, the normal retirement age for women who entered the workforce before 1996 is age 60. For those who began contributing to the program in 1996 or later, the normal age is 65 but benefits are payable as early as age 57.

8. L. 243/2004.

9. During each of these periods, the minimum retirement age for the self-employed will be one year later.

10. Currently, the normal retirement age for women who entered the workforce before 1996 is age 60. For those who began contributing to the program in 1996 or later, the normal age is 65, but benefits are payable as early as age 57.

REFERENCES

Bosi, Paolo, Elena Giarda, and Paolo Onofri. 2003. "Italian Budget Policy: A Long Run Overview." Paper 2 in *The Consolidation of the General Budget in Italy—Tools, Costs, and Benefits.* International Forum for Macroeconomic Issues research project. Tokyo: Economic and Social Research Institute, Cabinet Office.

Brugiavini, Agar, and Vincenzo Galasso. 2003. "The Social Security Reform Process in Italy: Where Do We Stand?" Paper prepared for the research workshop organized by the Michigan Retirement Research Center on International Social Insurance Reform, Ann Arbor, MI, July.

Brugiavini, Agar, and Franco Peracchi. 2004. "Micro-Modeling of Retirement Behavior in Italy." In *Social Security Programs and Retirement around the World: Micro-Estimation,* edited by Jonathan Gruber and David A. Wise (345–98). Chicago: University of Chicago Press.

Dang, Thai Than, Pablo Antolin, and Howard Oxley. 2001. "Fiscal Implications of Ageing: Projections of Age-Related Spending." Working Paper 305. Paris: Economics Department, OECD.

European Commission, Economic Policy Committee, Directorate-General for Economic and Financial Affairs. 2005. *European Economy: The 2005 EPC Projections of Age-Related Expenditure (2004–2050) for the EU-25 Member States—Underlying Assumptions and Projection Methodologies.* Special Report 4/2005, ECFIN/CEFCPE (2005)REP/55087. Brussels: European Commission, November.

European Commission, Economic Policy Committee, Working Group on Ageing. 2001. *Public Pension System Projections: Italy's Fiche.* Brussels: European Commission, August.

Ministero dell'Economia e delle Finanze. 2004. "Italy's Stability Programme: Update November 2004." Unofficial English translation. Rome: Ministero dell'Economia e delle Finanze.

Organisation for Economic Co-operation and Development. 2000. *OECD Economic Surveys: 1999–2000, Italy,* vol. 2003/13. Paris: OECD, May.

———. 2004. *Ageing and Employment Policies, Italy.* Paris. OECD.

———. 2005. *Pensions at a Glance: Public Policies across OECD Countries.* Paris: OECD.

Pisauro, Giuseppe. 2003. "The Central State Budget Process in Italy." Paper 3 in *The Consolidation of the General Budget in Italy—Tools, Costs, and Benefits.* International Forum for Macroeconomic Issues research project. Tokyo: Economic and Social Research Institute, Cabinet Office.

Pollnerová, Stěpánka. 2002. "Analysis of Recently Introduced NDC Systems." Prague: Research Institute for Labour and Social Affairs, December.

Samwick, Andrew A. 2003. Review of "Institutions and Saving for Retirement: Comparing the United States, Italy, and the Netherlands," by Arie Kapteyn and Constantijn Panis. Unpublished manuscript, Dartmouth, MA, July 26.

Toossi, Mitra. 2002. "A Century of Change: The U.S. Labor Force, 1950–2050." U.S. Bureau of Labor Statistics *Monthly Labor Review* 125(5): 15–28.

U.S. Social Security Administration, Office of Policy Data. 2005. *International Update: Recent Developments in Foreign Public and Private Pensions.* Washington, DC: U.S. Social Security Administration, December.

U.S. Social Security Administration, Office of Research, Evaluation, and Statistics. 2004. *Social Security Programs throughout the World: Europe, 2004.* SSA Publication 13-11801. Washington, DC: U.S. Social Security Administration, September.

Paul N. Van de Water

Clearly, we have "misunderestimated" the Italians. I am not refer-ring to the 2006 Winter Olympics, which ran smoothly. Rather, the Italians seem to have stabilized the long-run cost of their social secu-rity system, and in the process have cut current workers' pension wealth by about 40 percent. This type of fiscal macho should be enough to please even the deficit hawks at the Committee for a Responsible Fed-eral Budget.

Some observers contend that the Italians didn't suffer any short-run pain from the cuts and that they put off all of the pain until the long run. That turns out not to be true. In 1992, just before the reforms, public pensions in Italy took up 14.9 percent of gross domestic product. Today, the figure has declined to 14.2 percent. That accomplishment looks pretty impressive to me.

Moreover, the cost of public pensions as a percentage of gross domes-tic product is projected to go up only a bit between now and 2030—by about 0.8 percentage points—and decline again after that. Compared to other countries, however, Italy is not in such good shape, despite the sub-stantial cuts in pension wealth. What stands out is that the Italian system is still the most expensive in absolute terms.

What did the Italians do to achieve, if not fiscal sustainability, at least a substantial improvement in their fiscal situation? They have done a lit-tle bit of everything.

First, they changed the indexing of postretirement benefits, which formerly were adjusted by wages. Postretirement benefits are now being indexed by prices, and for high-income people, by less than prices. Second, the Italians increased payroll tax contributions. Third and most important, they restructured initial retirement benefits to improve work incentives. The earliest age of eligibility has been raised, the required years of contributions for benefits have been increased, replacement rates have been pared back at all ages, and incentives to retire early have been reduced.

As a result, analysts expect that the reductions in pension spending will be achieved primarily by lengthening work lives. If this is the case, additional earnings will help offset the benefit cuts and prevent significant reductions in lifetime income. This approach should gladden those of us who have contended for years that much more is to be gained by increasing labor supply than by promoting saving and investment.

Despite these improvements, my fellow economists can always find a cloud in any silver lining and a reason to rain on any parade. They raise at least three criticisms of the Italian reforms.

First, although work incentives have been improved, the reductions for early retirement are still less than fully actuarial, so an implicit tax on additional years of work remains. This criticism carries some force, but the problem would seem to be easily fixed, especially in the long run, when pension costs are projected to decline as a share of gross domestic product. Moreover, the 2004 reforms have moved the system in the right direction by increasing age and contribution requirements for the seniority pension, starting in 2008.

Second, some contend that the reductions are not being phased in quickly enough. But, as I noted earlier, costs are projected to rise only modestly over the next 25 years before starting to subside. This increase is hardly a great cause for concern. Moreover, most observers think that it was precisely the relatively slow phase-in that allowed these reforms to be put into place without overwhelming objections. In the same way, the U.S. managed to phase in an increase in the full retirement age by scheduling it to start some 20 years in the future. And, contrary to Maya MacGuineas, I do not think the change was hard to understand. I think that it was acceptable because it was put into place with a long amount of lead time.

A third complaint is that the funded second pillar is being phased in too slowly. Considering the generosity of the Italian system, however, I wonder if they need a second pillar at all. According to calculations made by the OECD and cited in the chapter, the Italian system will have a gross replacement rate of 79 percent and a net replacement rate of 88 percent in the long run.

If there is a problem with the Italian reforms, it is the one the authors mentioned. Namely, the automatic stabilizers do not seem to be fully effective, so adverse demographic or economic events can still require ad hoc corrections.

While no reforms are ever final, and while the Italian system will doubtless need further adjustments, the reforms appear from this distance to be nothing short of amazing. But why did the Italians take these dramatic steps? I still find the answer to that question to be a bit of a mystery.

Alicia Puente Cackley, Tom Moscovitch, and Benjamin Pfeiffer credit the impetus of the 1992 Maastricht Treaty. But the reductions in spending achieved both in the first 10 years and over the long run seem to go far beyond what might have been required simply to meet the Maastricht criteria.

The budget process rule the authors mention also doesn't sound like much of a factor. What they describe is something like a pay-as-you-go rule, which would constrain increases in spending, but which doesn't seem to be well structured to reduce spending.

Other authors cite Italy's 1992 foreign exchange and public finance crisis as a motivating factor. It occurred about the same time as economic crises in Sweden and in other European countries. One writer says that this crisis forced the unions to accept reform and that the Italian government was granted authority to reform the system within guidelines set by the parliament (Pennisi 2005). That is, the parliament didn't have to reach agreement on every detail of the reforms but left the government with considerable flexibility.

The 1992 reforms were parametric changes, designed to deal with a short-term crisis primarily by cutting spending, and therefore did not create a sustainable structure. That was left to the 1995 changes. But even those were put together hurriedly and enacted without extensive debate. Not surprisingly, therefore, more changes followed in 1997, 2001, and 2004.

Since many minor improvements still seem necessary, I think that we can expect further reforms. But, as the Italians say, Rome wasn't built in a day.

REFERENCE

Pennisi, Giuseppe. 2005. "Recent Pension Reforms in Sweden and Italy: The Notional Defined Contribution Approach." In *Workable Pension Systems: Reforms in the Caribbean,* edited by P. Desmond Brunton and Pietro Masci (177–216). Washington, DC: Inter-American Development Bank.

Dalmer D. Hoskins

N o one should apologize for not being an expert on the Italian pension system because there are very few experts, even in Italy. And I think a lot of people in Rome would like to keep it that way.

Italy is, however, one of the most important OECD countries economically, and it is a great pity that we do not know more about it, particularly because it has one of the worst demographic situations imaginable—as bad as Japan's. Somewhere around 2040, the number of Italians older than age 60 will equal the number of children in the population, a daunting challenge for the country's future.

And, along with Japan's, Italy's population will shrink in absolute terms as early as 2007. Unless birth rates change, there will be steadily fewer Italians than there are today, despite immigration (which is itself a big political issue there).

A report by the Center for Strategic and International Studies (Capretta 2007) ranks Italy as among the worst cases in its vulnerability to aging. Moreover, its people have readily taken to early retirement. They are, in fact, among the champion early retirees of all the OECD countries.

Keep in mind that early retirement does not necessarily mean that Italians stop working. One possible reason Italians have so readily accepted pension reform is that so many work off the books after getting their pensions. And so in Italy, more so than in many other OECD countries, people seem to accept as a fact of life that you get your pension and then work under the table. It is not that the Italians are less inclined to work; on the contrary, they are perhaps more creative in their retirement.

I also find absolutely extraordinary that Italians are exceptionally optimistic about their future. The European Union repeatedly produces a survey series called the EuroBarometer in which they ask people about their expectations for retirement. The Italians are among the most optimistic about how much they will be receiving and about how well they are going to be living. This shows that there can be little relationship between how people think about retirement and the financial reality of their national retirement income system—these are apparently two quite different matters.

Not being an expert in Italian social security, I did turn to some people who are. And the first person I called is a gentleman named Giovanni Tamburi, former head of social security at the International Labour Organization—a well-known international expert and an advisor for the recent Italian reform, which was largely conceived in the Ministry of Finance without any interference from the labor unions, the employers' federation, or even the social security institutions. All the usual players were thus largely frozen out of the reform process.

According to Tamburi, the Ministry of Finance was able to blame the need for pension reform on Brussels. The Ministry argued that it was all the fault of the European Monetary Union, which requires a country's public debt ratio not exceed 60 percent. The Italian experience provides an example of how an incredibly complicated structural reform can be shoved through a system without parliamentary approval of the details. Italy passed what they term a framework law, allowing the details to be worked out later by the various ministries and social security agencies. And so the reform constituted a profound change by introducing a version of the notional defined contribution system, inspired primarily by Sweden's reform.

Another close observer whom I consulted is my former colleague and an internationally known social security actuary, Warren McGillivray. Warren has written that "a consensus can involve such a complicated parametric modification to a defined benefit system that no one really understands it" (McGillivray 2007). And that is no doubt the case in Italy. The public reportedly understands little of what the reform actually entails.

Moreover, the reform is being phased in over such a long period of time that few have paid it the attention it deserves. And unfortunately, while fiscal solvency can be achieved in the long run, some severe short-term problems may meanwhile occur. Italy has tried to tackle the short-term problems, but the efforts ended in massive national strikes and the government backed off.

In Italy's 2006 elections, Silvio Berlusconi, the prime minister who spearheaded the pension reform, lost his bid for reelection to Romano Prodi. However, Prodi will be obliged to resume efforts to fix the pension system's short-term financial shortfalls. And he faces a politically difficult choice between injecting additional revenues into the pension system and sharply curtailing benefits, even for current beneficiaries.

Some aspects of the Italian reform have interesting implications for the United States. Italy has made energetic attempts to keep people working longer. Italians are retiring too early, and the increase in disability beneficiaries is among the most intractable problems facing Italy today. Some past years, in fact, saw more people going on the disability rolls than retiring. One innovation was to actually pay people to stay in the labor force between 2004 and 2007. Those who had already fulfilled the eligibility requirements for a pension but nevertheless continued to work were granted cash payments equal to their social security contributions. The payments were significant because they represented up to 32.7 percent of salary—equal to the contribution rate for the Italian pension system. Italy is among the few countries to experiment with giving people a cash payment, not just an increase to their pension, if they delay retirement.

Another distinctive feature of Italy's public pension system is the beauty of its default arrangements. Italians receive by law a whopping 7 percent of their salary in severance pay. The Finance Ministry has long thought that it would be far preferable for workers to use this severance pay as a supplementary second-pillar pension benefit. Private or employer-sponsored pensions in Italy have been underdeveloped in comparison with those of most of their European neighbors.

Thus, Italy passed a law in 2005 that aims to promote second-pillar pension arrangements. The money will go directly into one of three supplementary pension vehicles by default; workers will be obliged to opt out if they want to receive the severance pay in cash. Whether Italians will be happy with this new system remains to be seen. In any case, default options are being talked about in the U.S. as well, as a means to oblige people to save more for their retirement. For example, enrollment in such vehicles as 401(k) plans could be by default, since many more people have been shown to participate by default than would enroll on their own initiative (Iwry and John 2006).

So Italy presents a little-known but interesting case study because of the magnitude of its problems and the originality of its reform efforts. Do Italians understand what is happening? Will they remain as optimistic about their retirement? Perhaps not, but as with the British, the Italians will gradually begin to understand the gravity of the pension problem as their replacement rates begin to decline significantly.

As noted in Capretta (2007), Italy ranks in the OECD group as having among the worst rates of estimated poverty among the elderly. Future Italian governments will not escape the pressure to alleviate this growing crisis. So, in spite of the recent reforms, the public debate on pensions in Italy is far from over.

REFERENCES

Capretta, James C. 2007. "Global Aging and the Sustainability of Public Pension: An Assessment of Reform Efforts in Twelve Developed Countries." Aging Vulnerability Index Project Report. Washington, DC: Center for Strategic and International Studies.

Iwry, J. Mark, and David C. John. 2006. "Pursuing Universal Retirement Security through Automatic IRAs." In *Aging Gracefully: Ideas to Improve Retirement Security in America* (45–76). Washington, DC: Century Foundation Press.

McGillivray, Warren. 2007. "Evaluating Reforms in Social Security Protection." In *Social Security as a Human Right: Drafting a General Comment on Article 9 ICESCR—Some Challenges* (157–69), vol. 26, *Veröffentlichungen des Instituts für Deutsches, Europäisches und Internationales Medizinrecht, Gesundheitsrecht und Bioethik der Universitäten Heidelberg und Mannheim.* Berlin: Springer Berlin Heidelberg.

About the Editor

Rudolph G. Penner is a senior fellow at the Urban Institute and holds the Arjay and Frances Miller chair in public policy. Previously, he was a managing director of the Barents Group, a KPMG company. He was director of the Congressional Budget Office from 1983 to 1987. From 1977 to 1983, he was a resident scholar at the American Enterprise Institute. Previous posts in government include assistant director for Economic Policy at the Office of Management and Budget, deputy assistant secretary for Economic Affairs at the Department of Housing and Urban Development, and senior staff economist at the Council of Economic Advisors. Before 1975, Penner was a professor of economics at the University of Rochester.

He was elected president of the American Tax Policy Institute in 2005 and is past president of the National Economists Club. In 1989, he received the Abramson Prize for the best article published in 1988–1989 in *Business Economics* and more recently received a prize for the best article published in 2002 in *Public Budgeting and Finance*. In 2004, he chaired the Commission on Metro Financing for the Washington Metropolitan Area Council of Governments and others and recently chaired the Committee on the Future of the Fuel Tax for the Transportation Research Board of the National Academy of Sciences.

He is the author of numerous books, pamphlets, and articles on tax and spending policy and has authored columns for various newspapers including the *New York Times, Washington Post,* and *Los Angeles Times.* His most recent book, coauthored with Isabel Sawhill and Timothy Taylor, is *Updating America's Social Contract* (W. W. Norton & Company, 2000).

Penner's undergraduate degree is from the University of Toronto and his Ph.D. in economics is from the Johns Hopkins University.

About the Contributors

Alex Beer is the senior work, pensions, and education advisor at the British Embassy in Washington, DC, where she identifies and facilitates U.S.-UK best-practice domestic policy exchange. Previously, she worked as an economic advisor to the UK's Department for Work and Pensions. Recently she has specialized in pensions and older-worker policy, but she has also worked extensively on lone-parent, family-benefits, and child-poverty policy. Beer holds a master's degree in economics from University College London, and a bachelor's degree in philosophy, politics, and economics from Oxford University.

Réal Bouchard is general director of the Federal-Provincial Relations and Social Policy branch at Canada's Department of Finance. Bouchard has worked in Social Policy for more than 25 years, the last 10 as director. He has been involved in all the major reforms of Canada's social programs, including children's benefits, unemployment insurance, and pension reform, especially the Canada Pension Plan. As a member of the federal-provincial committee of Finance officials responsible for triennial reviews of the Canada Pension Plan, Bouchard has participated in all the reviews of the plan in the last 20 years. Bouchard has chaired the committee since 2000.

Stuart Butler is vice president for Domestic and Economic Policy Studies at the Heritage Foundation. He plans and oversees the Foundation's research and publications on all domestic issues. He is also an adjunct professor at the Georgetown University Graduate School and in 2002 was a fellow at Harvard University's Institute of Politics. Butler is author of *Enterprise Zones: Greenlining the Inner Cities* (Universe Books, 1981) and *Privatizing Federal Spending* (Universe, 1985), and coauthor of *Out of the Poverty Trap* (Free Press, 1987) and *A National Health System for America* (Heritage Foundation, 1989).

Alicia Puente Cackley is an assistant director in the Education, Workforce, and Income Security Team (EWIS) at the U.S. Government Accountability Office. Cackley received her Ph.D. in economics from the University of Michigan in 1990 and joined GAO as an economist in what was then known as the Human Resources division. As an assistant director in EWIS since 2000, she has managed several teams of analysts doing policy research on Social Security reform, retirement and aging issues more broadly, and immigration issues.

James C. Capretta is a fellow at the Ethics and Public Policy Center (EPPC) and an adjunct fellow with the Global Aging Initiative of the Center for Strategic and International Studies. From 2001 to 2004, Capretta served as associate director for human resource programs in the Office of Management and Budget (OMB). After leaving OMB, Capretta joined Wexler and Walker Public Policy Associates, where he served as a managing director until joining EPPC in August 2006. Prior to joining OMB, Capretta served for nearly a decade as a senior policy analyst for the U.S. Senate Budget Committee under Senator Pete Domenici (R-NM), handling health care and Social Security issues.

Jagadeesh Gokhale is a senior fellow at the Cato Institute. He works on entitlement reforms and U.S. fiscal policy generally. He is most well known for his work on the intergenerational redistributive effects of fiscal policy. In 2002, Gokhale served as consultant to the U.S. Department of the Treasury. Prior to that, he was a visiting scholar at the American Enterprise Institute for Public Policy Research and a senior economic advisor at the Federal Reserve Bank of Cleveland.

Dalmer D. Hoskins is senior managing director of policy at AARP. Previously, he was elected as secretary general of the International Social Security Association (ISSA). He has also served on the boards of the UN

International Institute on Ageing and HelpAge International. Hoskins begun his career in the Social Security Administration's Office of Research and Statistics and subsequently moved to the ISSA, where he became director of the Research and Documentation program. Between 1983 and 1990, he returned to the Social Security Administration, where he served as special assistant to the public trustees and director of the Office of Policy Development.

Neil Howe is a historian, economist, and demographer who writes and speaks frequently on generational change in American history and on long-term fiscal policy. He is cofounder of LifeCourse Associates, a marketing, human resources, and strategic planning consultancy serving corporate, government, and nonprofit clients. His coauthored books include *On Borrowed Time* (Transaction Publishers, 1988), *Generations* (Harper Perennial, 1991), *13th-Gen* (Vintage, 1993), *The Fourth Turning* (Broadway, 1997), and *Millennials Rising* (Vintage, 2000). He is also a senior associate at the Center for Strategic and International Studies, a policy advisor to the Blackstone Group, and a senior advisor to the Concord Coalition.

Richard Jackson is a senior fellow at the Center for Strategic and International Studies, where he directs the Global Aging Initiative; an adjunct fellow at the Hudson Institute; and a senior advisor to the Concord Coalition. Jackson's *Aging Vulnerability Index*, developed for CSIS, provides the first comprehensive and consistent measure of the aging challenge in developed countries. Jackson helped develop the National Taxpayer Union Foundation's National Thrift Plan, an early blueprint for a funded system of personal Social Security accounts. In 1994, he served as a liaison to the Kerrey-Danforth Commission on Entitlement and Tax Reform. He has also been a research fellow at the Hudson Institute, contributing to the pathbreaking Workforce 2000 project.

Estelle James is a consultant to the World Bank, USAID, and other organizations. Previously, she was lead economist at the World Bank and director of its flagship course on pension reform. She has also served on the board of Kosovo's new pension fund and the President's Commission to Strengthen Social Security in the U.S. She is principal author of *Averting the Old Age Crisis: Policies to Protect the Old and Promote Growth* (Oxford University Press/World Bank, 1994), the first global analysis of economic problems associated with population aging. Previously she was professor of economics and provost of social and behavioral sciences at the State University of New York, Stony Brook.

Tetsuo Kabe is counselor (Finance) of the Embassy of Japan, responsible for fiscal and tax policies and financial regulations. He has professional experiences encompassing public finance and fiscal sustainability issues, having worked in key positions of the Budget and International bureaus of the Ministry of Finance, the National Tax Agency, and the Office of the Prime Minister. As deputy director for Budget Review on Social Security and Social Welfare in the Budget Bureau, he was in charge of public pension reform and introduction of long-term care insurance. Kabe received his LL.M. from Harvard Law School and was visiting scholar at UCLA School of Law in 1988–1989.

Agneta Kruse is a senior lecturer in the Department of Economics, Lund University, Sweden. Kruse has also served as an expert for the Parliamentary Committee on Pensions, headed by Sweden's Ministry of Health and Social Affairs. The Swedish government appointed her to the National Social Insurance Board for a 1995–1997 term; since 1999, she has worked in their research division. She also serves on the Scientific Board of the Swedish Association of Local Authorities and with KEFU, a cooperation between local authorities in the Swedish province of Scania and Lund University. Her research focuses on social insurance, especially pensions and sickness insurance

Maya MacGuineas is president of the Committee for a Responsible Federal Budget and director of the Fiscal Policy Program at the New America Foundation. Her work has been published in outlets including the *Atlantic Monthly*, the *Washington Post*, the *New York Times*, the *Financial Times*, the *Los Angeles Times*, and the *Washington Monthly*. MacGuineas also helped craft Senator John McCain's Social Security reform proposal during his presidential campaign in 2000. Prior to that, she worked at the Brookings Institution, at the Concord Coalition, and on Wall Street. She received her master's degree in public policy from the John F. Kennedy School of Government at Harvard University.

Michael Mersmann is the former counselor of Labor and Social Affairs for the German Embassy in Washington, DC. Since 1982, he has been an officer in the German Mining, Chemical, and Energy Industrial Union (IG BCE). He has served on several supervisory boards, for Novartis GmbH,

Veba / BP Refining and Petrochemicals, Continental Can Europe, Buna AG, and Dresden Paper AG. He is chair of the IG BCE industrial policy group, and the chemical sector groups of the European Mining, Chemical, and Energy Workers Foundation and the International Chemical, Energy, and Mining Workers Federation. Mersmann is also vice chair of the German Chemical Professional Association.

Tom Moscovitch has worked at the U.S. Government Accountability Office (GAO) since 2004. He has contributed to reports about Social Security reform in other countries, wildland-fire cost sharing, and Medicaid waivers. Prior to GAO, Tom worked in finance for six years.

Edward Palmer is a professor of social insurance economics at Uppsala University and heads a division working with evaluation and modeling at the Swedish Social Insurance Agency. He was an expert in the Swedish government's Working Group on Pensions that formulated the Swedish pension reform and a member of the government's reform implementation group. He has worked as an advisor on pension policy for a number of governments and is the author of numerous publications on social insurance.

Benjamin Pfeiffer is a senior analyst in the Education Workforce and Income Security team at the U.S. Government Accountability Office (GAO). He received his master's of public administration from the University of Washington's Graduate School of Public Affairs and has worked for the GAO since 1984 on higher education, aging, and retirement issues.

Stanford G. Ross has served as chairman of the Social Security Advisory Board, commissioner of Social Security, and public trustee of the Social Security and Medicare Trust Funds. He has also served in the U.S. Treasury Department, on the White House domestic policy staff, and as general counsel of the Department of Transportation. Under the auspices of the International Monetary Fund, the World Bank, and the U.S. Treasury Department, he has provided technical assistance on social security and taxes to various foreign countries. Ross is an honorary advisor and founding member, and a former director and president, of the National Academy of Social Insurance.

Lawrence H. Thompson is a senior fellow at the Urban Institute and recently completed a term as president of the National Academy of Social Insurance. Thompson is also a consultant to the World Bank, the Asian

Development Bank, and the International Labor Office. Previously, Thompson was principal deputy commissioner of the U.S. Social Security Administration; assistant comptroller general at the U.S. General Accounting Office (GAO), responsible for oversight of federal health, education, labor market, and income security programs; and GAO chief economist. His most recent book is *Older and Wiser: The Economics of Public Pensions* (Urban Institute Press, 1998).

John Turner is a pension policy consultant. He is a member of the National Academy of Social Insurance, serves on the board of directors for the European Network for Research on Supplementary Pensions, is a fellow of the Pensions Institute (UK), serves on the editorial board for *Benefits Quarterly,* and for six years was chair of the pension committee on the Board of Pension and Health Benefits for the Baltimore-Washington conference of the United Methodist Church. He has authored or edited 12 books, most recently *Individual Accounts for Social Security Reform: International Perspectives on the U.S. Debate* (Upjohn Institute, 2006).

Paul N. Van de Water is vice president for health policy at the National Academy of Social Insurance. Previously, he served as assistant deputy commissioner for policy and associate commissioner for research, evaluation, and statistics at the Social Security Administration and assistant director for budget analysis at the Congressional Budget Office. While at CBO, he coordinated the analysis of the Clinton administration's health plan and other health care reform proposals. A founding member of the National Academy of Social Insurance, Van de Water has edited several Academy publications, including *Developing a Better Long-Term Care Policy* (2006), *Security for America's Children* (1992), and *Social Insurance Issues for the Nineties* (1992).

Index

accountability requirements in Canada, 14
Allowance (Canada) eligibility and bene-
    fits, 25–26
annuities
    factors as automatic adjustment mech-
        anisms, 58
    in Italy, private contracts for, 136–37
    Swedish FDC, 42
Asian currency crisis (1999), 76
ATP program (Sweden)
    benefits under, 36–37
    eligibility requirements for, 37–38
    phasing out of, 44
        projected expenditures on, 38
automatic adjustment mechanisms
    in Canada, 14, 32
    in Germany, 108
    in Italy, 149
    in Japan, 32, 80–81, 90, 91
    life expectancy and, 52*n*
    in Sweden, xii, 32, 39–40, 41, 58, 61
automatic enrollment. *See* default enroll-
    ment programs

Barr, Nicholas, 129
Basic Pension program (Japan), 71–74

Basic State Pension (UK), 112–13, 116,
    120, 123*n*
Beer, Alex, 111–25
Berlusconi, Silvio, 142, 153
Bouchard, Réal, 1–26
budget process
    in Italy, 141–42
    in Japan, 83–84, 93
    in Sweden, 47–49
Bush, George W., ix, 28–29
Butler, Stuart, 27–30

Cackley, Alicia Puente, 135–45
Canada, 1–26. *See also specific programs*
    Allowance eligibility and benefits,
        25–26
    Butler on, 27–30
    Capretta on, 31–33
    comparison with U.S., 4–6
    CPP. *See* Canada Pension Plan
    death benefits, 11, 23
    disability pensions, 2, 11, 22
    expenditures, public pension, 4
    factors in reform success, 11–15
    Guaranteed Income Supplement eligi-
        bility and benefits, 2, 3, 25–26

Canada (*continued*)
   immigration, role of, 31–32
   indexation of benefits, 24
   Old Age Security program. *See* Old Age
      Security
   private savings role, 2, 3, 4
   public consultations on reform, 12–15
      federal-provincial cooperation,
         14–15
      financing fairness, 12
      governance and accountability, 14
      investment policy, 13–14
      public nature of plan, 13
      reform success and, 16, 28
   public pension plans
      financing of, 6
      structure and parameters of, 21–26
   reform agreement (1997), 9–11
      benefits administration, 11
      financial implications of, 11
      funding increases, 9–10
      investment policy, 10
   reform pressures, 7–9
   Registered Pension Plans, 2, 4
   Registered Retirement Savings Plans,
      2, 4
   replacement rate, 2, 4, 5, 6
   retirement income system, 1–4, 11,
      21–22
   survivor benefits, 2, 22–23
Canada Pension Plan (CPP)
   contribution rates, xi, 9–10, 22
   current status, 15, 21, 22, 23
   Investment Board
      assets, 17n, 18n, 24
      creation of, 10
      independence of, 1
      return on assets, 15
   review process for, 15
   structure and parameters of, 1–2, 3,
      21–24
Capretta, James C., 31–33
Carter, Jimmy, 107
Center for Strategic and International
   Studies on aging population in Italy,
      151

children
   raising of
      Germany, pension contributions
         during, 98
      Sweden, pension credits for, 39, 46,
         48
      United Kingdom, 113, 114
   survivor benefits for
      Germany, 99
      Sweden, 43
Chile
   political sustainability of pension pro-
      grams in, 64
   price indexation in, 56
Clinton, Bill, 28
closed-period-balancing financial projection method, 81–82
collective bargaining agreements in Sweden, 51n
Commission for Sustainable Funding of
   the Social Security Systems (Germany), 97
Committee for a Responsible Federal
   Budget, 105
compulsory savings programs
   in Germany statutory pension insur-
      ance, 97–99
   proposals for, 105
Conservative Party (UK), 121
contracted-out pension schemes (UK),
   113–14
contribution rates
   Canada Pension Plan (CPP), xi, 9–10,
      22
   in Germany, 98, 103
   in Italy, xiii, 148
   in Japan, 83–84, 93
   in Sweden, 35–36, 47–49
CPP. *See* Canada Pension Plan

death benefits. *See also* survivor benefits
   in Canada, 23
default enrollment programs
   proposals for, 104–5, 153
   in UK, 120, 129

defined benefit plans. *See also specific plans*
 in Canada, 16
 in Japan, 71, 90
 reform challenges for, 105
 in Sweden, 36–38, 43, 50
 in UK, 117, 118
demographic pressures
 automatic adjustment mechanisms and, 32, 90
 in Canada, 7–9, 31
 in Germany, 108
 in Italy, 135, 136, 151
 in Japan, 69, 70, 74, 77, 79, 87, 95
 risks of changes in, 58
 in Sweden, 49–50
disability benefits
 in Canada, 22, 32
 in Italy, 136, 153
 in Sweden, 39, 48

early retirement age
 in Italy, 148
 normal retirement age versus, 65
Eberstadt, Nicholas, 31
economic pressures
 automatic adjustment mechanisms and, 32, 39
 in Canada, 7–9
 in Japan, 76–77
 risks of changes in, 58
Employees' Pension Fund (Japan), 72
Employees' Pension Insurance (Japan)
 age of eligibility for, 74, 75, 76
 benefits under, 71
 contribution rates, 91, 92
 creation of, 72
 funding for, 72, 83, 93–94
 reserve fund for, 94, 95
energy assistance program, 112
European Commission's Economic Policy Committee, 143
European Monetary Union, 138, 141, 149, 152

expenditures, pension plan
 in Canada, 4
 in Italy, 139–40
 in Japan, 77–78
 in Sweden, 35, 36, 36t, 49, 57
 in UK, 116–17, 124n
 in U.S., 4

federal-provincial cooperation in Canada, 14–15, 17n
fertility rate
 in Canada, 31
 in Germany, 108
 in Japan, 69, 74, 79, 95
 in Sweden, 58, 64
Finance Act (2004, UK), 118
financial defined contribution scheme (FDC, Sweden), 35, 42
financial projection methods, 81–82
Fiscal Structural Reform Law (1998, Japan), 76
folkpension benefits (Sweden), 36, 38
full-career labor force participation by women, 45–46
full-time/part-time labor force participation by women, 45–46

gender issues. *See* women
generational equity issues
 in Canada, 8, 9–10, 12
 in Germany, 109
 in Italy, 142
 in Japan, 82–83, 90, 91
 in Sweden, 42
Germany, 97–101. *See also specific programs*
 automatic adjustment mechanisms in, 32, 108
 Commission for Sustainable Funding of the Social Security Systems, 97
 comparison with U.S., 107–8
 contribution rates, 98, 103
 demographic pressures, 108
 fertility rate, 108

Germany (*continued*)
    Green Party generation in, 109
    Howe on, 107–10
    indexation of benefits, 108, 110*n*
    MacGuineas on, 103–6
    occupational retirement provision, 100
    old-age pension provision, 99, 100–101
    replacement rates, 108
    retirement age, 98–99, 103, 108–9
    Riester pensions. *See* Riester pensions
    Rürup Commission, 108
    self-employed persons, 101
    statutory pension insurance, 97–99
    survivor benefits, 99
    tax-assisted savings programs, 100–101
GIS. *See* Guaranteed Income Supplement
Gokhale, Jagadeesh, 87–90
Green Party generation (Germany), 109
Greenspan, Alan, 29
Guarantee Credit (UK), 114–15
Guaranteed Income Supplement (GIS,
    Canada), 2, 3, 25–26
guarantee pension (Sweden), 38, 43,
    44–45, 48

health care
    in Japan, 71, 85*n*
    in Sweden, 46–47
    in UK, 132
    in U.S., 132
higher education, pension credits for, 39,
    48
Home Responsibilities Protection (UK),
    113
Hoskins, Dalmer D., 151–54
housing supplement benefits (Sweden),
    43, 48, 49, 57
Howe, Neil, 107–10

immigration, effect of, 31–32, 95
indexation of benefits
    in Canada, 24
    in Germany, 108, 110*n*
    in Italy, 148

    in Japan, 76, 80–81
    to life expectancy, 130
    price versus wage, 57
    in Sweden, 37
    in UK, x, 114, 115, 116
individual accounts. *See* privatization of
    public pension plans
infinite-horizon unfunded liabilities, 88
*An Information Paper for Consultations on
    the Canada Pension Plan* (Canada),
    8
inheritance gains, 39, 52*n*
inkomstpension. See notional defined con-
    tribution (NDC) scheme
insurance annuities. *See* annuities
investment policy in Canada, 10, 13–14
Italy, 135–45. *See also specific programs*
    Amato reforms, 138, 139, 140, 142
    Berlusconi reform proposals, 142
    budget process and political climate,
        141–42
    contribution rates, xiii, 148
    demographic pressures, 135, 136, 151
    Dini reforms, 138, 140, 142
    disability benefits, 136, 153
    early retirement in, 148
    EU entrance criteria and, 138, 141,
        149, 152
    expenditures, pension plan, 139–40
    historical background, 136–37
    Hoskins on, 151–54
    indexation of benefits, 148
    mandatory old-age insurance, 136–37
    notional defined contribution (NDC)
        accounts, 138, 139
    Pension Reform Act (2004), 141
    private insurance annuities, 136–37
    reforms, 137–42
    replacement rates, 148
    retirement age, 138, 148
    severance payments, 137, 141, 153
    supplementary pension systems,
        136–37
    survivor benefits, 136
    system dependency ratio, 135, 136,
        143

Trattmento Fine Rapporto (TFR), 137,
    143*n*
Van de Water on, 147–49

Jackson, Richard, 91–96
James, Estelle, 55–60
Japan, 69–86. *See also specific programs*
    automatic adjustment mechanisms in,
        32, 80–81, 90, 91
    Basic Pension program. *See* Basic Pen-
        sion program (Japan)
    budget process, 83–84
        cash deficits in, 93
        expenditures, 83, 84
        revenues, 83, 84
    closed-period-balancing financial pro-
        jection method, 81–82
    comparison with U.S., 87–88
    demographic pressures, 69, 70, 77, 79,
        87
        projections for, 74, 95
    economic pressures, 76–77
    Employees' Pension Fund, 72
    Employees' Pension Insurance. *See*
        Employees' Pension Insurance
    expenditures, pension plan, 77–78
    fertility rate, 69, 74, 79, 95
    financial projection methods, 81–82
    GDP growth in, 73
    generational equity issues, 82–83, 90,
        91
    Gokhale on, 87–90
    immigration to, 95
    indexation of benefits, 76, 80–81
    infinite-horizon unfunded liabilities
        and, 88
    Jackson on, 91–96
    labor force participation rate, 79, 95
    life expectancy, 74–75, 79
    Mutual Aid pensions, 71
    National Pension System, 71, 73–74
    plan funding, 83–84, 93
    private pension systems, 72
    public communication of reforms,
        82–83

public long-term care insurance sys-
    tem, 71, 85*n*
public medical care insurance system,
    71, 85*n*
public pension systems, 71–72
    actuarial evaluation and review of,
        78–80
    compulsory enrollment for, 72
    historical background, 72–73
    mandatory reviews of, 78–80
reforms, 72–78
    of 1985, 73–74
    of 1994, 74–75
    of 2000, 75–77
    of 2004, 77–78
replacement rates, 81
retirement ages, 95
Social Insurance Agency, 78
social insurance system in, 71–72
Social Security Council, 79, 82
system dependency ratio, 92
whole-future-balancing financial pro-
    jection method, 81–82

Kabe, Tetsuo, 69–86
Kohl, Helmut, 107
Kruse, Agneta, 35–53

labor force participation
    automatic adjustment mechanisms
        and, 39
    gender differences in, 37, 45–46
    in Japan, 95
    in Sweden, 37, 45–46, 50
    in UK, 118
    labor unions and contractual benefits
        in Sweden, 51*n*
    life expectancy
        automatic adjustment mechanisms
            and, 39, 52*n*
        gender differences, 46
        in Japan, 74–75
        in Sweden, 37, 39, 40, 58, 64
long-term care insurance in Japan, 71, 85*n*

Maastricht Treaty of 1992, 138, 141, 149
MacGuineas, Maya, 103–6
mandatory old-age insurance (MOA, Italy), 136–37
McGillivray, Warren, 152
medical care. *See* health care
Medicare (U.S.), fiscal challenges of, 64–65
Mersmann, Michael, 97–101
military service, pension credits for (Sweden), 39, 48
Missfelder, Philipp, 109
Moscovitch, Tom, 135–45
Mutual Aid pensions (Japan), 71

National Health Service (UK), 111
National Pension Savings Scheme (UK), 120
National Pension System (Japan), 71, 73–74
National Welfare Board (Sweden), 49
normal versus early retirement age, 65
"The Northern America Fertility Divide" (Torrey & Eberstadt), 31
notional defined contribution (NDC) scheme
   in Italy, 138, 139
   in Sweden, xi, 35, 38–42, 55–56

OASDI. *See* Old-Age, Survivors, and Disability Insurance
occupational pensions
   in Germany, 100
   in UK, 115
Occupational Pensions Regulatory Authority (UK), 118
Old-Age, Survivors, and Disability Insurance (OASDI, U.S.), 4, 17*n*
old-age pension provision (Germany), 99, 100–101
Old Age Security (OAS, Canada)
   eligibility and benefits, 25–26
   financing of, 6
   structure and parameters of, 2, 3, 24–26

Palmer, Edward, 35–53
parental leave benefits (Sweden), 39, 48
part-time labor force participation by women, 45–46
Penner, Rudy, 85*n*, 92
Pension Commission (Sweden), 36
Pension Credit (UK), 112, 114–15, 116
pension credits (Sweden), 39, 46, 48
Pension Protection Fund (UK), 118
Pension Reform Act (2004, Italy), 141
pensions. *See specific countries and types of plans*
Pensions Act (2004, UK), 118
Pensions Bill (2006, UK), 122–23
Pensions Commission (UK), 119, 128, 129
Pensions Regulator (UK), 118
Pfeiffer, Benjamin, 135–45
political sustainability
   in Canada, 12
   in Italy, 141–42
   pension program sustainability and, 64, 66
   in Sweden, 51
   in UK, 64, 120–21
   in U.S., 29
PPM. See Premium Pension Authority (Sweden)
premiepension. See financial defined contribution scheme (FDC, Sweden)
Premium Pension Authority (*PPM,* Sweden), 42, 47
price indexation of benefits, 37, 57
private pension systems
   in Canada, 2, 3, 4
   in Japan, 72
   in UK, 115, 117–18, 122–23
privatization of public pension plans
   in Canada, 13
   Greenspan on, 29
   in UK, x, 127
   U.S. proposals for, 28–29, 32–33
Prodi, Romano, 153
provincial-federal cooperation in Canada, 14–15, 17*n*

public consultations
    in Canada, 12–15, 16
    in Japan, 82–83
public long-term care insurance system
    (Japan), 71, 85*n*
public medical care insurance system
    (Japan), 71, 85*n*
public pension systems. *See also specific*
    countries or plans
    in Canada, 4, 6, 21–26
    government borrowing from, 6
    in Japan, 71–73, 78–80
    political sustainability and, 65–66
    privatization of. *See* privatization of
        public pension plans

Québec Pension Plan (QPP), 1–2, 3, 17*n*
    reform measures, 14–15

ratio of pensioners to workers. *See* system
    dependency ratio
redistribution effect, 6, 38, 50
Registered Pension Plans (RPPs,
    Canada), 2, 4
Registered Retirement Savings Plans
    (RRSPs, Canada), 2, 4
replacement rates
    in Canada, 2, 4
    gender differences, 45–46
    in Germany, 108
    in Italy, 148
    in Japan, 81
    in Sweden, 44–47
retirement age
    in Germany, 98–99, 103, 108–9
    in Italy, 138, 148
    in Japan, 95
    normal versus early, 65
    in UK, 129
retirement plans. *See specific countries and*
    types of plans
Riester pensions (Germany), 97,
    100–101, 104, 105, 109
Ross, Stanford G., 127–30

RPPs. *See* Registered Pension Plans
    (Canada)
RRSPs. *See* Registered Retirement Savings
    Plans (Canada)
Rürup Commission (Germany), 108

Savings Credit (UK), 114–15
savings rate
    in Japan, 90
    in UK, 118
self-employed persons
    in Germany, 101
    National Pension System (Japan) for,
        71
    in Sweden, 47
    in UK, 111–12
severance payments in Italy, 137, 141,
    153
Social Insurance Agency (Japan), 78
Social Security (U.S.), private investment
    proposals for, 28–29, 32–33
Social Security Council (Japan), 79, 82
SSI. *See* Supplemental Security Income
Ståhlberg, Ann-Charlotte, 45
State Earnings-Related Pension Scheme
    (SERPS, UK), 113
State Second Pension (UK), 113–14, 123*n*
statutory pension insurance (Germany),
    97–99
Steuerle, Gene, 92
Sundén, Annika, 45
Supplemental Security Income (SSI,
    U.S.), 4
survivor benefits
    in Canada, 22–23
    in Germany, 99
    in Italy, 136
    in Sweden, 43
Sweden, 35–53. *See also specific programs*
    ATP benefits. *See ATP* program
        (Sweden)
    automatic adjustment mechanisms in,
        xii, 32, 39–40, 41, 58, 61
    budget process, 47–49
    comparison with U.S., 57

Sweden (*continued*)
  contractual benefits under collective
    bargaining agreements, 51*n*
  demographic pressures, 49–50
  disability insurance benefits, 39, 48
  expenditures, public pension, 35, 36,
    49, 57
  financial defined contribution scheme,
    35, 38, 42
  folkpension benefits, 36, 38
  guarantee pension, 38, 43
    funding of, 48
    indexation of, 48
    price indexation effect on, 44–45
  housing supplement benefits, 43, 48,
    49, 57
  impact of reforms, 43–47
  indexation of benefits, 37
    price versus wage, 57
  James on, 55–60
  labor force participation, 37
    gender differences in, 45–46
    retirement age and, 50
    of women, 37
  life expectancy, 37, 40
  National Welfare Board, 49
  new system, 38–47
  notional defined contribution. *See*
    notional defined contribution
    (NDC) scheme
  parental leave benefits, 39, 48
  Pension Commission, 36
  pension credits, 39, 48
  plan funding and contributions,
    35–36, 47–49
  political issues, 51
  Premium Pension Authority, 42
  previous system, 36–38
  reform pressures, 49–51
  replacement rates, 44–47
  retirement age, xi, 40
  survivor benefits, 43
  unemployment insurance benefits, 39,
    48
Swedish Social Insurance Agency, 40

system dependency ratio
  in Italy, 135, 136, 143
  in Japan, 92
  in Sweden, 41

Tamburi, Giovanni, 152
tax-assisted savings programs
  in Canada, 2, 3, 4
  in Germany, 100–101
  in UK, 115
  in U.S., 30
10-year labor force participation by
  women, 45–46
Thompson, Lawrence H., 61–67
Torrey, Barbara Boyle, 31
Trades Union Congress on compulsory
  saving (UK), 121
traditional insurance annuities (FDC,
  Sweden), 42
Trattmento Fine Rapporto (*TFR,* Italy),
  137, 143*n*
Turner, John, 127–30

unemployment insurance benefits (Sweden), 39, 48
United Kingdom, 111–25. *See also specific*
  programs
  automatic enrollment programs, 120,
    129
  Basic State Pension. *See* Basic State
    Pension (UK)
  Conservative Party in, 121
  contracted-out schemes, 113–14
  expenditures, pension plan, 116–17,
    124*n*
  Finance Act (2004), 118
  Guarantee Credit, 114–15
  health care provisions, 132
  Home Responsibilities Protection, 113
  indexation of benefits, x, 114, 115, 116
  labor force participation, 118
  National Health Service, 111
  National Pension Savings Scheme, 120
  occupational pensions, 115

Occupational Pensions Regulatory
    Authority, replacement of, 118
Pension Credit, 112, 114–15, 116
pension principles, 119
Pension Protection Fund, 118
Pensions Act 2004, 118
Pensions Bill (2006), 122–23
Pensions Commission, 119, 128, 129
Pensions Regulator, 118
plan funding, 116–17
political sustainability of pension pro-
    grams in, 64, 120–21
private pension savings, 115, 117–18,
    122–23
privatizing social security in, 127
reforms, 118–20
retirement age, 129
Ross on, 127–30
Savings Credit, 114–15
savings rate, 118
self-employed persons, 111–12
State Earnings-Related Pension
    Scheme (SERPS), 113
state pensions and benefits, 111–15,
    122
State Second Pension, 113–14, 123*n*
system sustainability, 115–18
tax-assisted savings programs, 115
Turner on, 127–30
Winter Fuel Payments, 112
women and pension eligibility, 123
United States
    automatic adjustment mechanism pro-
        posals for, 62
    comparison with Canada, 4–6

comparison with Germany, 107–8
comparison with Japan, 87–88
comparison with Sweden, 57
"double indexing" in, 107
expenditures, public pension, 4, 131
health care costs as barrier to reform,
    132
indexation of benefits in, 66
political issues with reform, 29–30
public consultation on reform, 28–29
replacement rates, 5, 6, 108, 131
retirement age increases in, 65
Social Security, private investment
    proposals for, ix, 28–29, 32–33
wage inequality as barrier to reform,
    59
unit-linked insurance annuities (FDC,
    Sweden), 42

Van de Water, Paul N., 147–49
voluntary carve-out accounts, 127–28.
    See also privatization of public pen-
    sion plans

wage versus price indexation of benefits,
    57
whole-future-balancing financial projec-
    tion method, 81–82
Winter Fuel Payments (UK), 112
women
    labor force participation gender differ-
        ences, 45–46, 95
    in UK, pension eligibility of, 123